The L Word

How I Beat the 2020 Pandemic with Humor

By Jerry Perez

Index

Introduction   **5**

Chapter 1: Laugh (Observational Humor)   **9**
- A Whole New World   **10**
- I Hate Tuesdays   **11**
- Old Dogs… New Tricks   **12**
- Mother's Day   **14**
- Vodka, Underwear Models & Other Things I Keep in My Basement   **16**
- And for My Next Trick…   **17**
- Holy Progress, Batman!   **19**
- September (A.K.A. The Jan Brady of Every Year)   **20**
- Halloween   **22**
- Gay Sex   **25**
- Thanksgiving, No Thanks   **27**
- I Want My Fruitcake & Eat it Too…Maybe…Not Really   **29**
- Yay, Christmas!   **31**
- Cheers!   **32**
- New Year's Resolutions   **34**
- Baby Talk   **35**
- I Need a Vacation from Vacationing   **36**
- On with the Show!   **37**
- Life is a Party   **38**
- New Car, Guys in my Trunk & a Little Fabric Softener   **40**
- Riding the Relation-ship   **42**
- To Shave or Not to Shave… That is the Question   **44**
- A Life to Remember   **46**
- Valentine's Day (A.K.A. One of the Reasons I drink)   **48**
- Things I Never Want to Hear Ever Again   **50**
- Alternative Titles to Famous Movies   **51**
- English to Grindr Dictionary   **53**
- 50 Things I'd Rather Do   **55**

- I'm Getting Old **57**
- The Wrong Things at the Wrong Times **58**
- Nightmare TV Ads **60**
- Buy Coffee if You Dare **64**
- Anger Management **66**
- The Vaccine is Here! **68**
- DC Comics **71**
- I Rather be Blue than Yellow **72**
- The Extra Mile **73**
- The Angry Chiwawa **74**
- Give Me a Break! **75**
- If I Could Turn Back Time **77**

Chapter 2: Learn (Cooking, Crafts & Things) **78**

- The Chocolate Coma **79**
- Unicorn Poop Cookies **80**
- Easy Crème Brûlée **81**
- Ham & Cheese Croissant Casserole **83**
- Pavlova Recipe **84**
- White Chicken Chilli **86**
- Ice Cubes **88**
- Chocolate Bunnies **89**
- Punishment Dinner **90**
- Wrapped Up Children **91**
- Chilly Cheese Dogs **93**
- How to Make Paper Roses **94**
- I Saw the Sign **99**
- SAD Party **101**
- Memoriam Roast **103**

Chapter 3: Live (Social Media) **106**

- Reasons Why Nobody Ever Goes Shopping with Me **107**

- Reasons Why I'm Not Invited to Things   **108**
- Blah Blah Blah…   **109**
- The Wonders of Text Messaging   **161**
- Random Conversations with Random People Chosen at Random   **163**
- Random Randomness   **165**
- Meme Time   **168**
- Baby Yoda ®   **172**

Chapter 4: Love (Poetry)   **176**

- Thanksgiving Poem   **177**
- My Obsession   **178**
- iDicted   **179**
- Crazy Cat Carlitos   **182**
- Look at Me!   **182**
- Fried Love   **183**
- Mother Spellcheck   **183**
- My $ecret Love   **185**
- Why English is Hard to Learn   **186**
- Simply Papers   **187**
- So Close. Yet So Far   **195**
- The Last Poem   **195**
- My Birthday Wish   **197**
- Live!   **198**
- New Year's Poem   **199**
- The Pink Sheep   **199**
- I'm Sorry   **200**
- I'll Show You!   **202**

Chapter 5: Lure (Bucket List)   **203**

In Conclusion   **215**

About the Author   **217**

Introduction

I haven't lived a long life, so I am in no position to talk to anyone about what the meaning of it is. I wouldn't be able to teach youngsters about all the hardships of life, getting married, having a family, building a home, reaching old age or becoming a long-range shooter for the CIA. But if anyone needs assistance tying the stem of a cherry in your mouth without using your hands, I'm your man!

The pandemic we faced in the year 2020 made me feel like a complete loser. I used to be an event and wedding coordinator, but social gatherings were not permitted anymore due to the COVID-19 virus. I got another job selling vacation packages over the phone (Telemarketing, which is a degree you earn at Darkest Deepest Corner in Hell University. Go Devils!), but no one was flying or cruising anywhere to avoid contagion, so sales weren't doing so well. Then I worked for a restaurant which made me a victim of cutbacks they were forced to have due to lack of business. I had just broken up with someone after a 4-year relationship due to constant arguments about the bills amongst other things and we also lost our home because we couldn't afford payments. I was also trying to quit smoking at this time. It is needless to say the world was not safe around me at this point in my life! Kicking a defenseless puppy and making babies cry brought me no shame (not that I tried these things, but I started to not care about myself or others).

My ex-boyfriend and I were lucky to have our families helping us with food and money. After we ended our relationship and moved out of our home, I decided to move back to the Caribbean (which is where I'm from) to live with my mother. We both needed each other at this time. I needed all the help I could get! She was having many medical complications and I had to be sure she was helped with anything she needed before retiring. She has been there for me every day of my life for many years, so it was only fair I took one year off my life to dedicate entirely to her.

So yeah… the year 2020 was not our year, but I decided to do something constructive with my time. I began to help mom with tending and fixing her house before selling it. I did the catering for all her meetings with her colleagues at work, did the cooking and cleaning in her house which was as big as a baseball field (I really wish I was kidding about that), did the laundry, and cared for our dogs. She also got me to see a psychiatrist due to my depression and anxiety. At the end of the day, I still had 9 to 13 hours in a day to waste, which I spent in a big empty house alone dealing with silence while mom was at work. She is a doctor and had only one rule during this pandemic: NO ONE IS ALLOWED INSIDE THE HOUSE. That did wonders for my depression! Our whole lives, we are taught to believe it is better to be sociable and fun rather than an antisocial wallflower. This year was an extrovertive person's nightmare! Here we are now walking up to introverts asking "how the hell do you do it? Teach me your ways, oh powerful lonely one!"

On a side note, I also want to express my condolences to the friends and families of those who have fallen due to this horrible virus we faced during this year.

Do you want to know what my "cure" for depression caused by COVID-19 was?

HUMOR!

"I want to make the world laugh!" - is what I told my parents from a very early age, which made them worry about my financial future. I don't even know where I got a sense of humor from. Everyone in my family is a doctor and I am the pink sheep of the family who turned out to be a gay writer with aspirations of working in the hospitality (not "hospitals") industry and literature. You know that kid who was always passing out funny notes in class when we were in school? That was me. One time, the teacher caught us, confiscated the note and asked who the perpetrator was. They all pointed at me. Thanks a lot, guys! She asked if she could take the note with her to show the other teachers because she thought it was very funny and made her laugh. We all laughed, so ever since that day, others began taking the credit for these notes! I started signing them with my name and added an ® symbol next to it as if I was sending something that was copyrighted. Sometimes I would be asked to see the principal, but other times it brightened our days. This was back in the year nineteen-ninety-bad when our Wi-Fi had an annoying internet dial-up noise, bracers where only metallic and Google® consisted of going to a library and actually reading a real book. Kids today see a book on the floor and start to poke it with a stick trying to figure out what this strange object is.

I published books on horror-fiction, self-help, and then I suffered a car accident which caused me to lose my memories including the ability to speak, walk, or write. I had to relearn everything again and it was a very difficult and long journey. I also used to write a comedic column for a local magazine for seven years and I was always the one people counted on to make their days brighter with a joke. The thing is… clowns never get a day off. You're not allowed to have a bad day because the world relies on you to make them laugh. No one is there to make you laugh when you are the joker. This led to a lot of anxiety and depression. I had co-workers who would literally call me to say "are you scheduled to go to work today? Because my father died last week and I feel like crap, but I know you can make this day go by a lot faster". I've also participated in open mic nights at the local bars in South Florida to do standup routines. One drunken stranger came up to me and said "you better make me laugh, clown because I had a horrible day today at work and my girlfriend dumped me". No one cared I was mourning the death of my dog that day or that I also had a difficult day at MY job. My sister is the only person who could always make me laugh hysterically! Mom laughs at her own "jokes" to the point she's in tears while we look at each other wondering what just happened. - "Mom, are you going to be OK?". They were never funny at all, but we loved seeing her laugh so intensely because of these.

I noticed that, on social media, members of my family, group of friends, and others would give each day of the week a purpose or a reason to do something just as long as the activity started with the same letter of the alphabet of that particular day of the week. So, I had people wishing me a happy "Workout Wednesday" and "Throwback Thursday" where I get to workout and share my baby pictures with friends and a bunch of strangers on social media.

While living with my mother, I hated to look at myself in the mirror feeling sorry for myself without anything to do and no one to talk to making me feel like a complete loser. Then I started to look for other words that started with the same letter as the word "loser" so that I can turn something negative into something positive. The first thing that came to mind was "learning" as

I've always been a huge nerd, a fan of literature and a comic book geek, so I thought of learning new things that I didn't know before. I began to study ASL (American Sign Language), how to make paper flowers, and cooking. I utilized social media to speak to people from all over the world and learn about their cultures and holidays. I have 46 new friends from Europe, Asia, Africa, South America, the Caribbean, Canada, and the United States I need to meet in person at this point.

The term "hashtag" is utilized to refer to those activities that are attached to the day of the week that starts with the same letter of the alphabet. Just to name a few, there is, as mentioned before, Throwback Thursdays or #TBT, #ManicureMonday, #TastyTuesday, #WineWednesday, #FridayFun, #SweatSaturday and #SelfieSunday. But for me, all my days consisted of working out every day of the week! The reason? I moved to the freaking Caribbean! Almost everything we cook is fried. A typical breakfast consisted of fried eggs with fried cheese, fried sausage, fried bacon, fried plantains… we were one step away from frying the orange juice too! My gut slowly started to become the death of my penis.

So, with the help of a psychiatrist, medication, and a lot of wine, I was able to stay more positive and looked up more words that started with the letter "L" to combat my feelings of being a "Loser". I chose every vowel to follow this letter and that's how my journey with this book began: La, Le, Li, Lo, Lu.

The LAUGH chapter is based on observational humor in essays I have written. I just pretended to be talking to a friend about anything that came to mind. Since I couldn't have anyone in my house and had to keep my distance from others when going outside that left me with the only obvious option: talking to the bees in a beehive we had in the backyard. But they had no interest in talking to me. I guess the queen was offended because, not only was I not dressed to meet royalty in person, I also said to her "Bitch, I'm the only queen in this house!" – which was very offensive. Naturally, I apologized to her, but it was of no use. So, I tried apologizing again with a can of bug spray. That was the end of my social life as I knew it. Since I was in no hurry to see the inside of a mental institution, I decided to pretend I was speaking to a friend I imagined being in front of me in the hopes I could make him/her laugh with anecdotes. Hopefully, you can also find this chapter humorous.

The LEARN chapter is composed of things I learned during my exile such as ASL, how to make paper flowers, and cooking recipes from others.

The LIVE chapter is composed of humorous things I found on social media (which became my life during this period). I have a wacky group of friends and I always thought our conversations and pictures sent to one another to brighten our days could do the same for others, so I decided to share these with all of you on here. This pandemic alienated us from each other, and we were all going through difficult times in our lives individually, so I made it a mission to make people smile in every conversation we had with each other through text messages and social media.

The LOVE chapter is filled with poems about things we love. There is WAY too much hatred and negativity in the world, so I wanted to focus on love poems. Not just the love we have for one another, but poems about other things we love (even cake!) making a few of these very comical.

The LURE chapter is basically a list of 40 things we should do before we die. Why 40? I don't know… I mean, why not 27 or 15 or 386? Just accept it. Obviously, there are hundreds of thousands of things we can do, but this is MY list of things I wish I could do in the hopes to lure others into also having the same fun experiences. The difference between my bucket list and others in existence is that I am encouraging you to try these at least once a year for every year of your life as opposed to making a bucket list that would last you all eternity to finalize.

Well, I hope you enjoy reading this book just as much as I enjoyed creating it for all of you. This was the product of a pandemic that forced me to stay indoors with very little to do. I just wanted something positive to come out of something so tragic. I've always said that a smile on your face is your way of telling the whole world "is that the worst you can do?" Here we are still together, standing tall (unless you're short like me) and living our lives finding happiness wherever we can find it because that is the true meaning of life: to be happy and make others happy around us. So, go ahead, I dare you to laugh a little, learn a little, live a little, love a little more, and try to have new experiences in life before this is taken away from us.

Enjoy and be kind to bees!

LAugh

Observational Humor

A Whole New World

The world I thought I knew makes no sense to me anymore due to this pandemic we are facing. COVID-19 they call it.

We grow up reading comic books and loving masked heroes who save the world in many adventures but complain about wearing masks that could help us save one another. Wearing surgical masks and social distancing have been strongly encouraged to avoid contagion, but many people refuse to follow these rules increasing the number of reported infected cases and deaths. Because of my asthma, I am at a higher risk to contract it than others, so I must be extra careful. Now, it's a norm to wash all your groceries after you buy them or have them delivered to your house, wash your hands 100 times a day and avoid contact with everyone around you (even family members who don't live in your household)! Suddenly, going to a restaurant will cause your friends to alienate you forever!

Aside from this virus, we have other strange behavior we have witnessed for years! I know there are women who wouldn't want to date or sleep with a man who sleeps with and dates other women at the same time. But these are the same women you hear at work talking about how awesome The Bachelor® TV show was last night. This is a show in which we see one man dating multiple women at the same time as they share the same living space to talk about their dates with this man. What?!

I am friends with Black people who hate hearing the word "nigger" or "the N word" as it's preferably called, yet they blare it out when it's used in a rap song they like thinking it's a whole different thing when pronounced differently. "It's OK when I say *nigga*!" – they say to me. In that case I can be called a "spac', because "spic" is too racist? Get serious! If there is a word we don't want to see or hear ever again, it must be completely eradicated from our language!

You see gay men who would like to get married and have a family someday hoping it changes the way gay stereotypes are seen and live a peaceful normal life, yet I go on dating apps and other social media apps speaking to the same guys who are there looking for the "D" and engaging in recreational drug use.

When it comes to presidential elections, I know people who say they support and respect me as a Hispanic man yet vote for a man who doesn't. Women demand equality and some vote for the same misogynist prick, and gay people want respect, but also vote for the openly homophobic candidate.

Like I said before, the world stopped making sense. Strap on! It's going to be a bumpy ride!

I Hate Tuesdays

"I hate Mondays" – is what Garfield®, the cat is known for saying. I think Tuesdays are worse that Mondays. Tuesday's are life's way of saying "I don't think you suffered enough yesterday at work…here, have a crap-load of Tuesday"! If Monday is a car accident, Tuesday is the insurance company saying you're not covered. If Monday is a box of delicious chocolates, Tuesday is the doctor saying you're a diabetic. Monday is that guy who understands you are recovering from the weekend and says "are you ok? I know it's hard, but we'll get through this" as he hands you a cup of delicious coffee. Tuesday is the dude who says to you "I'm going to need you to redo that report from yesterday in German and I'm going to need that double-spaced. Is that clear"? If Monday makes love to you, Tuesday is the guy who jams his fist up your butt moving it around as if searching for a lost ring inside a garbage disposal because Tuesday is clearly a Monday with a vengeance. I'm not sure if I made my point clear but, in case you missed it, I freaking hate Tuesdays!

I'm writing this during the month of November, so get ready to hit those gyms to make room for the food orgy you are about to host inside your stomach during the many Thanksgiving dinners you will be invited to. I cannot wait! It has been a while since the last time I had a self-induced coma. Not to mention the ever-unavoidable family disputes about critical important issues such as who voted for whom on the last election or which friends of the family are getting a divorce. I am pretty sure they will ask me (once again) how I knew I was gay. When you're gay they always ask how this happened or if you are being safe when having sex with other men or if you have developed a fascination for leather yet. When you're straight the questions vary a tad: "Are you seeing anyone?", "Is she cute?", "When are you getting married and having babies?"

I am not sure I remember the first time I realized I was gay. I think I remember my mother crying and my father and others around them wearing surgical masks and handing each other cigars. Then, this doctor grabbed me from my mom's cavernous dark hole where I spent my days in solitary confinement for nine months and showed my face to her yelling out "It's a boy"! I was born with headsets on as I listened to Madonna's "Holiday" and kept thinking how everyone wearing a scrub needed a serious makeover. I'm pretty sure that's when I found out I was gay. To most people, it was at the time of their teenage years or first crush. To me, it was immediately after that doctor spanked me because, instead of bursting into tears, I just turned my head to him and gave him a big wink and called him "daddy".

Nah! Just kidding! I came out just like every decent Catholic boy: it was announced in a courtroom as I was suing my priest for touching me inappropriately after mass. Well, I hope you all have a great Thanksgiving with your loved ones, and I hope it doesn't land on a Tuesday.

Did I forget to tell you how much I hate Tuesdays?

Old Dogs... New Tricks

Maybe some dogs are too old to learn new tricks. I have been training my pups to stay on their own bed at night and yet, every morning I wake up looking like Dr.-freaking-Doolittle with both dogs on me, a cat, a snake, a tarantula, and a goldfish... all of them fighting me over the damn blanket! By the way, it is important to mention that I only own two dogs, so I don't know where in God's green Earth the other ones came from! If you own pets, don't let them climb on your bed. It creates bad habits and a preconceived notion about boundaries. They end up thinking they own the place...that is until it's time to pay the rent, then it's YOUR place again.

Speaking of bad habits... I know music is an expression of the soul, but what is up with people dedicating songs to express how they feel? You want to tell him he's a cheap skate... you tell him you 'don't want no scrub'. You want to make him drop his current boyfriend for you, then you tell him you 'wanna be his girlfriend' and when all else fails and there are not enough words in the English language to express your inner most treasured emotions, then there's always 'Who Let the Dogs Out®?' I had an ex who once dedicated Bryan Addams' "Please Forgive Me®" to me.

"Please forgive me... I not know what I do.
Please forgive me, I can't stop loving you..."

Oh, I see... I guess this explains why you've been stalking and calling me incessantly for months after cheating on me. How sweet... Bryan Addams says "please, forgive me" 15 times in this song. There's a red flag right there! What did you do, Bryan Addams to deserve this punishment? What did you do, sir?! Now, thanks to my ex, every time I'm at the local bar and someone plays this tune in the jukebox, I run out with my hands in the air screaming: "Oh my god, someone PLEASE forgive him already!!!" At least, have the balls to apologize in person for what you have done. A recorded CD will not do the trick. But that's today's culture for you.

Also, there are so many foreign films out there with challenging subjects, not-so-happy yet necessary endings and courageously explicit climatic scenes. Unfortunately, most of these movies never get the exposure they deserve because, many of us, don't like subtitles! This is the struggle I go through with my friends:

"Let's watch this flick. It's from Russia".
-"Is it dubbed"?
"No"
-"Wanna go out somewhere they speak English?"

It's like trying to give pills to a dog! "This movie has a great message, but unfortunately it's Swedish with English subtitles... Mmmm, let's wrap it in bacon". Do you think films like Crouching Tiger Hidden Dragon® or Life is Beautiful® would've made the cut unless Hollywood made a big deal about them? It wasn't until their Oscar nominations that a mass production of dubbed versions of these films were produced. And when they are not dubbed, then we have to spend millions of dollars to recreate already-perfect movies into their "American versions" so that we can watch them in this country. Now 'Ringu' becomes 'The Ring', 'Let the Right One In' becomes 'Let Me In', and 'La Femme Nikita' becomes 'Point of No Return'.

People, there's a world out there that produces good films, TV shows and great music just like we do! Find them, learn something new and get ready to be entertained. Would you like me to teach all of you dogs out there a few new tricks? Here you go: SIT!…WATCH THIS SPANISH FILM!… AND STOP HUMPING MY LEG!

"every morning I wake up looking like Dr.-freaking-Doolittle with both dogs on me, a cat, a snake, a tarantula, and a goldfish"

Mother's Day

I'm going crazy looking for the perfect Mother's Day gift for my special lady! What can I give the woman who has it all? And even if she didn't have it all, there's nothing she ever wants, because she's all about "your happiness is all I want" until her eyes pop out of their sockets when we pass by that dress at Neiman Marcus®.

We have already given them so much! There are the stretch marks, the years of dirty laundry and all the food we made them prepare to give them a little distraction. Yeah…You're welcome, mom! Maybe we can give them a nice bottle of wine. After all, we are the reasons they drink anyway. They carried our sorry butts for 9 months physically and for 25 years financially, so they are entitled to a nice Mother's Day card. Unfortunately, they ran out of the ones that read "Happy Mother's Day! Sorry I wrecked your vagina on the way out". Speaking of childbirth…Ahhhhh! I feel sorry for women. Eve takes one little bite off an apple and women are doomed to a lifetime of monthly (bloody) visitors, 9 months of cravings with mood-swings and given the task of granting the gift of life by transforming her naughty parts into a passageway to Narnia® which it's used to push babies out in pain while choking their husbands' throats and screaming: "YOU DID THIS TO ME! GET ME DRUGS NOW!!!" (sigh…) Such a beautiful miracle indeed.

One of the things I find very interesting is the ability to pinpoint which women are mothers by the things they say. I know we all have experienced the following:

1. Eat your vegetables.
2. Go to your room.
3. This will hurt me more than it'll hurt you.

Of course, if you happen to have been raised by a Latina mother, you can add these to the list (notice the exclamation point at the end of every statement as I'm sure these were shouted at you):

1. ¡Te calmas o te calmo! (Calm down or I'll make you calm down!)
2. ¡No me molestes ahora que estoy viendo mi novela! (Not now, I'm watching my soaps!)
3. ¡¿Cómo que no vas a comer?! ¡¿Con tantos niños muriéndose de hambre en Africa?! (What do you mean you're not going to eat?! There are so many kids dying of hunger in Africa wishing they had what you have?!)

Why do they always bring the kids in Africa to our attention? I never understood that one. And who can forget the hours of "chismes" (gossiping) with the neighbor or worse…our sworn enemy…La Chancleta (this is their sandal which they always use as a weapon against us)?! (Cue eerie music). For those of you who don't know, *"la chancleta"* or *"la chancla"* (cue eerie music again) is a device utilized by Latina moms to correct their kids' behaviors, teach them the values of good conduct and aid them in the task of making good decisions. There are many myths regarding the origin of such item, but I'll share the real facts with you: A long time ago, a woman spoke to God claiming she was desperate to have her children listen to her and respect her. God advised her to sit with them and speak in a tender and loving manner. That obviously worked out as well as finding parking at a mall on a Saturday morning. In her despair, the woman spoke to the devil who gave her a device she could mask as an article of clothing and use as a boomerang when needed to cause great pain yet granting her the respect she craved through the fear and anguish of others. So, there it is…*la chancla* is nothing but a sandal hand-crafted by the devil himself for our Latina mothers to use on us causing us great pain when we misbehaved. And there are no child protective service agents who have ever been involved in their destruction because they are above the law apparently. Ok, maybe I'm exaggerating. I wouldn't want people to thing Latin-American mothers are physically abusive!

All that aside, our mothers deserve our love and devotion for always being there for us. For making our illusions come to life by becoming Santa Claus, the Easter Bunny and Tooth Fairy. For being there for us when we were in trouble or smacking us on the head when we got in trouble for not listening to their advice making us sit front row to their "I told you so" performances for hours. For always being present at every school play, every nightmare scare, every doctor visit, every graduation, every wedding, and every moment in our own children's lives to spoil them rotten as all grandmothers do. There are many things we aspire to become or to have as adults, but when we were kids, there was nothing we ever needed because we had it all…we had mom. I hope you always have many happy Mother's Days and, for Christ's sake, eat your vegetables!

"Sorry I wrecked your vagina on the way out"

Vodka, Underwear Models & Other Things I Keep in My Basement

Hello fellow readers! Well, it seems another summer is here! I hope you all worked hard on those beach bodies you were supposed to have by now. I worked really hard to get my summer body and all it took were a few glasses of Vodka, a $5,000 check and the promise of a Paris vacation. And this is how I got this Andrew Christian® underwear model trapped in my basement. What? Isn't that how you get a beach body for the summer? Were you expecting me to tell you about the diet I went on and the hundreds of hours spent at a gym trying to get muscular for the summer? If you were, I'd have to remind you not to mix alcohol with pain killers and high expectations.

I shouldn't have to worry too much about sweating so much during the summer to lose weight and, excuse me for sounding so conceited, but I am SO hot! I don't mean that in the way my underwear model "guest" in my basement would say it. I mean it's hotter than Santa Claus' crotch while walking the Sahara Desert for 2 days straight. People keep asking me to come up with things they can do during the summertime, but I cannot think of anything else that does not involve me laying naked inside a tub filled with a million ice cubes or bathing naked on the beach or walking around the house naked or walking…the dog…naked…? Hey…maybe I just really like being naked. That would explain why I always make neighbors so uncomfortable or people at the supermarket. Nah! That could not be the reason. I'm sure it's all those wonderful hats I wear. They're just jealous!

I hope you all had a great Mother's Day in the company of your mothers, aunts, and friends. I have this crazy lady who keeps confusing me with her son! She's always following me! Jeez lady! Your photos of me as a child and you holding my birth certificate or your strange resemblance to me will do nothing! Better try harder next time and no, I don't have bad memory so stop saying that I do.

Anyway…

What were we talking about?

Oh yeah! Father's Day! I wish I could have the time to spend it with my own father, but he stepped out to get cigarettes. He said he'll be back by 4:00pm. It is 4:15pm now so that makes him about 12 to 15 years late since he left the house years ago! That store must be REALLY far away!

Sometimes I get paternal myself, so I adopted a puppy dog for when those things happen. I already taught him how to sit and bark on command. Next week, I am going to teach him how to do the dishes and take out the garbage. The real reason why I got him was to act as a guard dog to do simple things such as protecting myself from unwanted intruders or making sure underwear models trapped in the basement don't escape. I'll get to those things in a minute, in the meantime, I hope you have a Happy Father's Day, Happy Gay Days at Disney World®, Happy Summertime and Happy Dirkmaticoulenshabby Day! It's just a day I created when I run out of reasons to drink and celebrate. Happy Dirkmaticoulenshabby Day, everyone! Cheers!

And for My Next Trick…

Ok, I want you to pick a card. Try to imagine a card…any card and I will attempt to guess what you chose. Got it? Is it the Queen of Hearts? I knew it! Ta da! And for my next trick…Bryan, the guy I met at the store last week. But if you want a more exciting trick…One Magical Weekend® in Orlando is finally here! This is a gay-themed weekend sponsored by many businesses and organizations housed at Disney World® among other locations in the Orlando area. It's going to be so magical! No magic shows have better "tricks" than that! For those of you who didn't know, a *trick* is a name we give to a one-night stand.

I'm looking forward to go to the Disney® theme parks. It may seem childish, but we would not be the fabulous queers we are now without our childhood heroes and heroines…Thumper, the rabbit (Mr. You Can Call Me Flower if You Want To), the Disney villains like the fabulous Cruella de Vil and her fur coats, the seductive Ursula with her tentacles all wrapped around poor little Ariel, Uncle Scar from The Lion King, and the captivating Evil Queen with her apples. That reminds me, I need to pay my phone bill…you know…because it's an iPhone®? …manufactured by Apple Inc®…? Never mind.

There are a few things I am definitely looking forward to like bathing in the pee-flavored pool water at the pool party in Typhoon Lagoon® and declaring bankruptcy after closing my tab at the nightclubs. Regardless, it's good to have events like these where we can be who we are without fear. Then again, there's also Pride Parades on Gay Pride Month, Gay and Lesbian Film Festivals, The Gay Olympic Games, grocery stores, your local bank and pretty much everywhere! Yes, indeed times are changing, but where else would you be able to hold your partner's hand as you walk around wearing Mickey Mouse® ears without people thinking you are some kind of child predator?

I know that many parties will be a lot of fun. These are great opportunities to meet new people, dance your butt off and wake up the next morning next to someone whose name you may not remember.

Did you know One Magical Weekend® is one of the largest GLBT events in the world?! The only thing bigger than that is my phone bill…which I just remembered again I need to pay at once. Is it GLBT or LGBT or GLBTQ or GWTF? I don't know, but it sort of made me hungry for a BLT sandwich now.

For those of you who are new to this experience and would like to be a part of this, I'd like to offer some help. Here are a few things you will probably need to know about it and by "probably" I mean "absolutely unnecessary":

1. Lines to get into rides inside the park are as inevitable as a buffet inside a cruise. Invest in a Fast Pass®. You'll be glad you did.
2. **Rest**rooms are not for **rest**ing.

3. When you invite friends or someone you've met into your home, do not have pictures of yourself all over because they'll think you're conceited. Replace those with pictures of me instead! Because, you know, I am not conceited.
4. If you forget someone's name, I have the best error-proof way of finding that out without looking bad. Simply look at them in the eye and say: "How did you say your name was spelled again?" & hope it's not Tom or Amy.
5. Using the phrase "you go, girl!" can be annoying to some. And girls may think you're actually asking them to go away.

Well, that's it for me. I hope these help you. And, by saying that, I mean "don't take me seriously". I do hope you have a fantastic experience with friends and loved ones. Be safe, wear condoms, look both ways before crossing the street and stay away from expired foods. Now if you all excuse me, I have to go now. There's something I know I had to do, but now I can't remember what that was. All I know is that I have to pay some sort of bill. I'm going to have to grab my phone and call my best friend. He always keeps me in check.

Using the phrase "you go, girl!" can be annoying to some. And girls may think you're actually asking them to go away

Holy Progress, Batman!

I went to the premiere of the hottest hit this season… Batman: The Dark Knight Rises®. Because of the title, I thought it was a bi-racial pornographic movie at first until I saw Batman on the screen. I saw it twice and stood in line for hours to see it because I'm that big of a nerd. By that statement you can deduce I don't get laid much. I was impressed with all the technology they showed on the screen. It makes me look into the technological advances we enjoy today. The things you can do with your cell phones alone today are amazing?! What did we do before smart phones came out? Oh, that's right… we had good memory, met people face to face and went to libraries to look for information. I don't think I know anyone who doesn't have a cell phone today. Even when I went to LA I met a homeless guy with a Bluetooth device. Leave it to LA to have that. I thought he wasn't really homeless. I thought maybe he was going 'Tyra Banks' on us and was doing a social experiment, but then I realized the blue tooth was the ONLY tooth he had, so… yeah I guess he was homeless after all.

I always have bad luck with technology. My GPS sucks! It always says useless crap like "your exit was back there" or "keep going forward, continue on this road" about six or seven times while driving down the highway. I proposed an idea to a friend of mine. Why can't we have a Mom GPS (MPS). I would imagine it would say things like "You were supposed to turn at the light. You never listen! This is why you'll never mount to anything" or "Your destination is on the right… Speaking of destinations, when are you finally getting married?" or "Would you like me to call AAA for you? While you're at it, think of why you don't call me more often? Did you know I had surgery last week? No, you know why? Because you're an ingrate!"

Some people however have an overwhelming addiction to technology. There are those who cannot live without their cell phones. Nothing aggravates me more than people who feel the need to answer a call in the middle of a movie…let's say for lack of a better example, the Batman premiere which I waited in line for hours to see and bought tickets 3 months in advance!!! It gets me so angry my only wish is to gag them, dress them up like an empanada and tie them to a post in Cuba. They won't leave a trace! I know I shouldn't get angry and practice to turn the other cheek, but isn't it easier to turn THEIR cheeks with a fist? Yes, I could kill them with kindness, but wouldn't a knife get the job done faster? Maybe I'll have a knife in my pocket and call it *Kindness*. I'm getting off track, I know… and a tad too aggressive.

Don't get me wrong, I like technology. In fact, just like the MPS idea, I've had others, but they didn't quite make the cut such as my glow-in-the-dark sunglasses, inflatable dart boards, waterproof towels and my helicopter ejector seat idea. I guess I should keep my daytime job.

Regardless of the technological advances we enjoy today, remember every once in a while, to write a letter instead of a text message, shake a hand instead of 'poking' someone online and enjoy a dinner and a movie with someone you'd like to meet as opposed to sending a picture of your naughty spots on dating phone applications.

September (A.K.A. the Jan Brady of Every Year)

Man! I honestly don't know what to say about the month of September! What is September famous for other than leaves turning colors as they dry up and Labor Day? Actually, did you know that the name "September comes from the Roman Latin *'septem'* for seven, since this was the seventh month of the Roman calendar? I don't really have a joke for that. Just thought you'd like to know that.

Well, vacation time is about to begin for me. I understand why people would want to travel to awesome places in summertime such as California or Cancun or New York, but I live in that state which cannot make its mind as to whether be the state with the most beautiful flowers that grow out of the most beautiful homes' landscaping or be the state with the most landscapers or children of such. You guessed it…Florida. The land of game show hosts daring you to drive a car that has been parked under the hot sun for hours or have an outdoor wedding in June! The winners get to take a long shower with freezing water. I believe there are some places in the world that use the expression "go to Florida?!" as the equivalent to saying "go to hell?!" It is beyond my understanding why people pick summertime to come to Florida to walk for hours in the theme parks and wait in long lines under the hot sun to hop on a ride. "This ride is about 6 minutes long and the wait time for your turn is about 2 hours...totally worth it!"

Have you ever heard of Ithyphallophobia? It is the morbid fear of thinking about or seeing penises.

Nothing?

Uh…well, I guess there are no jokes about that either.

I just realized it is not only September, but I am also writing a piece on this deadbeat month on a Tuesday! Yes, people… Freaking Tuesday which is the week's biatch! Garfield made Mondays famous by simply hating them, we get to hump on Wednesdays and then go to church on a Sunday to ask for forgiveness due to the massive humping just mentioned, we then share old photos of ourselves on Thursdays (#TBT), and then we have TGIF. Tuesday? Where's Tuesday? Have you seen it? I cannot find it anywhere! Oh, that's right, I forgot Tuesday is that week's middle child who just threw a rope around its neck and jumped off a ten-story building because it knows you like "the other kids" more.

Oh! Here's another interesting fact… US dollar bills are made out of cotton and linen…

Cotton… and linen…

Nope, still got nothing!

Many friends have invited me to do the "foodie thing" so now we get dressed up to go to restaurants we've never been to before and make comments on the YELP® app in our phones. But there is a different option to that and I like to call it ABSOLUTELY ANYTHING ELSE. This activity has caused me to develop a split personality disorder. There's this voice in my head that urges me to eat everything in front of me. This is my inner fat girl whom I like to call Felicia (for some reason). Now I have my friends yelling things at me like "No, Felicia! That's a bad Felicia!" every single time I try to nibble on some homeless old woman's arm. Don't even give me that look of disgust on your faces as you judge me so harshly while reading this. You act as if no one has tried that once or twice before. Yeah, right! Give me a break! I should get more into the habit of trying more American dishes because I realized how I've never had stuffed peppers or the classic green bean casserole. As a Latino man, there might have been many American foods I haven't tried but I must say that, in return, God granted me an amazing tan (modesty apart).

So… the average raindrop falls at 7 miles per hour and my interest in writing a piece about this month of September falls at 20 inches per second.

And that, ladies and gentlemen was my last attempt at talking about something interesting other than the month of September. Damn it! When is October coming along? Everybody likes October because it's fun and unpredictable. But not you, September. Everybody hates you. Go home, you lousy month! You suck, September! That is, of course, unless your birthday happens to be on this month in which case it is the coolest month of the year!

Byeeeeee!

"Have you ever heard of Ithyphallophobia? It is the morbid fear of thinking about or seeing penises"

Halloween

My favorite month of the year is finally here! A month to celebrate the beauty of the fall and all kinds of spooky things. Speaking of spooky, have you noticed how the news talk about Donald Trump every day! I hear about him so much I think it's influencing my need to turn a little bit racist. I mean, that would explain why my white bedsheets are hooded and have holes in them now as if needed to be used to see through them.

I'm guessing, by the way I present myself to you on this page, you may think the most elaborate and hard-to-pull-off costume I can wear for Halloween is dressing up like a decent human being. Well, I've got two things to say to you! First of all, how dare you?! And, secondly, you are absolutely right. Let's not forget it's that time of the year again in which we are faced with things we fear such as monsters, and Trump supporters with loaded firearms! I once had a fear of spiders and it was bad. I remember once seeing a spider in my tub, so I took the necessary precautions: grabbed a piece of tissue paper and then, very carefully and ever so gently, I burned the house down! I also had a fear of the dark, but that ended rather quickly this past summer once I opened my last electric bill. Now I'm afraid of the light.

Halloween was very confusing for me as a child. All my life my parents said, "Never take candy from strangers". Then October 31st comes, they dressed me up in a costume and said, "Go beg for it!" I didn't know what to do! I'd knock on people's doors and go, "Trick or treat" and then, as soon as people came out with the candy, I would say - "I can't. Sorry, I'm not allowed to accept that". But folks, there is nothing funny about Halloween. This macabre festival is nothing but a festival of children's demand for revenge on the adult world. I should know… I've done horrible things to neighbors. You know how kids would throw toilet paper on houses and trees? Well, I did the same thing. Only I discovered throwing grenades was a much better way to really ruin someone's day!

Regardless of what you end up doing this Halloween season, remember to always be safe, look both ways before crossing the street and do not put anything in your mouth unless it's wrapped! The same can be applied as dating advice.

I hope it doesn't rain like last year. I was completely nude and went as a man who just stepped out of the bath with bubbles covering me. OK, fine, I confess! I didn't have time to think of a good costume to wear, so I just stepped out of the bath and walked down the street. There! Are you happy?! I'm a pervert! I think this year I'll wear an Arnold Schwarzenegger mask. The best part? With a mouth full of candy, I will sound just like him.

I always say "clothes make a statement. Costumes tell a story". What'll be your story this year? Still don't know what to wear? No problem! I'm here to help. Here are some great costume ideas for you, guys:

1. Dress up as you normally do. If someone asks what you are, tell them you're a werewolf. If they ask why you have no hair or fangs, explain that it's not a full moon yet. Let's hope this is the case up above.

2. Put on a chicken costume and throw a leather jacket and helmet and you are a biker chick.
3. Wear a t-shirt with a large "X" on it and hold a knife in your hand and you're a crazy ex.
4. Use safety-pins to attach a bunch of cheap watches and jewelry on the inside of your coat. Go as a con man (or Wynona Rider coming out of a store).
5. Cover your face in white paint, wear a white wig and put on a white trash bag as clothing. You are now white trash. Don't forget the beer, the cigarette and the NASCAR cap.
6. Get a large box. Cut a hole for your head and arms. Wrap it with gift wrapping paper and put a big bow on your head. Make a large gift tag out of construction paper that reads: "To: All Men, From: God." This year, you can honestly say you're God's gift to men (or women).
7. Wear all black and a pair of dark sunglasses, or glasses with a rubber nose. Get a strip of fabric you can fashion into a sash (like a beauty queen's) and use fabric paint markers to write, "Bless you," across it. You're a blessing in disguise.
8. Wear a black catsuit and randomly attach different kinds of single socks all over you. You're the mysterious sock thief from the dryer. Trust me, it DOES exist!
9. Wear all pink and say you're a piece of bubble gum or a man who just came from a Gay Pride parade and had everybody throw up all over you.
10. Attach gum wrappers, soda cups and popcorn and you are a movie theater floor. Use hairspray to cover your entire body for that "sticky feeling".

But I'm in Puerto Rico right now and it's too hot to wear a costume. Unless I go as...

11. A Newborn Baby: walk around naked with a rope tied to your waist posing as the umbilical cord.
12. Michelangelo's David: walk around naked and cover yourself with only the leaf from a tree. Be sure to workout A LOT!
13. A Medieval Times Heretic: walk around naked with your arms wrapped behind you with a piece of rope. It helps if you have a buddy walking behind you holding a bible and pointing at you as he yells "SHAME! SHAME! SHAME!"
14. A Spoiled Indecisive Teenage Girl: walk around naked with your hair or wig in pig tails and suck on a lollipop as you yell out "I just can't find a thing to wear! Daddy! Help!"
15. The Victim of a Robbery: walk around naked yelling out "somebody call the police"! State some people robbed your car, took your wallet and your clothes.
16. A Tornado Survivor: walk around naked and state it was REALLY windy.
17. A Sport Fan Streaker: just walk around naked same as you would do for a Man Getting Out of the Shower costume and a Nudist costume.

Notice how they all begin with "walk around naked"? I'm telling you… it's VERY hot down here!

I have been to Halloween Horror Nights at Universal Studios in Orlando twice already, but the real fear is going to a Disney park and paying over $100 for a one-day ticket… or anything for that matter. I bought a shirt there once and had to use the title of my car as collateral!

Regardless of what you decide to dress up as or where you decide to celebrate Halloween, remember to be safe and have a great time!

All my life my parents said, "Never take candy from strangers". Then October 31st comes, they dressed me up in a costume and said, "Go beg for it!"

Gay Sex

I had the most interesting conversation with a friend of mine the other day. He was instructing me on several fetishes that some people practice, and he decided to tell me about all of this at 9am…

…in front of people…

…in church…

… We are no longer friends.

Seriously though, I was very intrigued and so impressed by a lot of things many of you may be experts on. I have never been that adventurous. To me, switching to the left hand when I'm having a "personal fun time" is a thrill.

One of the things we talked about was people getting aroused by doing #2 on someone. They call that 'scatting' (not the singing, unfortunately. Unless someone goes to the bathroom on your face as they go "do da di badi badi bada"!) Obviously, I told him how gross that was (if I offend anyone I apologize and I suggest you shower more regularly than others…Oh! And seek Jesus). "Don't knock it until you try it" – he said to me. Seriously?! I have crapped my pants before and that brought me nothing but discomfort and shame. Also, that was the last time I was ever invited to someone's birthday party.

He also explained to me about the concept of a "master/slave" relationship and told me he once was in training to be a sex slave. "Training?!" – I said to him – "Like he taught you how to sit and gave you a cookie? And what do you mean you wanted to become a slave?! Aren't you Black?!" Then he showed me a video of someone masturbating inside a cup of freshly cut fruit for another person to eat it covered with that layer of "baby juice" on it. These fetishes are getting weirder and more complicated as years pass. It's not just about making sure we have the right lighting in our bedroom anymore. Now you have to put plastic all over your room making it look like a murder scene is about to take place there! It's all so dirty now!

But who knows? I am starting to think that I may be into S&M (sadomasochism). I didn't even know pain got me aroused until I had a very heavy dumbbell fall on my foot at the gym and started limping out of there as I kept screaming out loud: "Holy s**t! I'm so freaking horny right now"!

I started an account on this phone app that facilitates sexual encounters with other men in your area because, you know, nothing bad could ever come out of that! There is a segment in which you must determine what your body type is or the type of guy you are. I found it peculiar how the gay community has gone from "muscular", "skinny" and "overweight" to what resembles nothing but a zoo. Nowadays we have "bears", "pups", "pigs", "otters", "cubs", etc. I'm sure many more animals will be making an appearance in those things. I know there are people who are attracted to overweight men with small penises. All it will take is one of these individuals to say "yeah, I'm hung like a hamster, baby"! – and BOOM! Now we have "hamster" in the list of types of men.

I've always been nicknamed after anything short and tanned because of my appearance. I've been nicknamed Scrappy Doo (because I also believe I can take on anyone and I have a big mouth that always gets me in trouble). My real name is Gerardo, but it is unpronounceable to most people who cannot roll the R's to make the sound my name requires, so I've been Jerry since college (after the cartoon mouse). Some call me Batman because I'm always trying to "save the world" and help others without superpowers.

Whatever you decide to call me, please don't refer to me as a hamster. I'm short, not little! There's a difference, believe me (wink, wink).

"Holy s**t! I'm so freaking horny right now"!

Thanksgiving... No, Thanks

Gobble, gobble, guys! I survived yet another Thanksgiving this year. I decided to pay respect to the ancestors by going "old school", so I broke into my neighbors' home and claimed it my own. Then I went through their pantry and ate all the food they had. I didn't invite them to share the delicious meal I prepared, but told everyone that I had. My friends were all so moved by what they thought I did; they decided to celebrate with their families every year on that same day in honor of my "generous" actions. Seriously, guys... let's celebrate this holiday the way our ancestors did and instead of filling our children's heads with that whole "Indians and Pilgrims came together to feast"- crap, let's eat our neighbours' crops and play a spirited game of Pin the Arrow on the Pilgrim's Heart. I don't mean to be a sour puss, but do I really have to pretend I care about this holiday yet another year? Most people don't even know the history behind it or why they celebrate it. We all act like robots around this time. A command triggers in our circuit when November comes along and everyone's walking around mouthing, "MUST-FIND-TURKEY!"

Oh, well... I guess there are many things I could be thankful for. I am thankful for gymnasiums and all the hot boys that make it impossible for me to not stare when they are working on those squat thrusts. Incidentally, I am also thankful for squat thrusts and penicillin. I am thankful for cell phones that have allowed me to never have to use my brain to remember ANYTHING ever again. I am also thankful for chocolate. My pants may never fit me again and I may punch a mirror every time I see how my clothes look on me, but you are still the most delicious thing on this Earth, chocolate! And lastly, I am thankful for anti-depressants without which I wouldn't be able to have a cheerful disposition during the holidays year after year. I'm sorry guys, I said I was not going to be a sourpuss and I did anyway. I will just leave my anger where it really belongs...at the dinner table with my family.

Now, why on Earth does my Latino community celebrate this holiday? I don't remember any pilgrims inviting us to share a meal with them, do you?! Would you like to know why we were not invited? Because they know how we roll. They knew that if they had invited us, we would have shown up with 5 other hungry Latino friends without an invitation! But that does not stop us from celebrating it. Leave it up to us to find yet another Holiday which will give us an excuse to over-eat again. If it was an all-American home cooked meal, maybe I wouldn't have to suffer the horrible consequences that come after in the restroom toilet (or as I like to call it, "the embarrassing sound amplifier for your butt"). But no, we have to cook the pork, the arroz con frijoles, the fried yucca, the plantains, tostones, empanadas, morcillas and turrón among many other heart-stopping dishes. This year I was ready for it! I took all the necessary precautions and gave my body a two weeks' notice: went to the gym to work out, took my vitamins, checked my blood pressure, got an MRI, drank protein shakes, got a physical, and went on Mapquest® to find the nearest hospital.

Why is eating a lot of food so grossly celebrated in our culture? There was a time I didn't question it and that usually happened when I met a new boyfriend and brought him home to mommy for Thanksgiving. We ALL have been there. We tell him or her on the way there: "You better eat whatever mamá puts on your plate and it wouldn't hurt to get seconds either". Unfortunately, the eating doesn't stop at her house; we have to go to Marías house because she invited us weeks ago and she has a new baby we must meet, then we have to make a stop at the boss' house because you really want that promotion and so forth. Last Thanksgiving, I went to so many houses even Santa Claus was amazed at how much mileage my car had. But gas prices are getting so high every day! Even drive-by shootings are minimizing because gang members can't seem to hate anyone hard enough to want to spend $20 on gas to put a bullet through someone's head. I sense an increase on bike-by shootings soon.

Not only did I survive Thanksgiving, but I also lived through another Black Friday. Only in America, people will trample over others for sales exactly hours after being thankful for what they already have!

But I did it anyway!

There are only two things in life that bring a smile to my face: cuddling on the couch to a classic movie and the look on people's faces when I elbow them in the eye as I dart to get that last iPad® on the rack.

"My pants may never fit me again and I may punch a mirror every time I see how my clothes look on me, but you are still the most delicious thing on this Earth, chocolate!"

I Want My Fruit Cake & Eat it Too… Maybe… Not Really

I am being severely punished as I am attempting to finish this fruit cake someone gifted me. I don't understand why people STILL insist on giving these as presents!

I guess this is just one of those things that defy explanation. Fruit is good… cake is delicious… Now put them together and you get two pounds of the most horrible thing ever eaten!

But I do love Christmas! One my fondest memories of the holidays back home was always having this sense of beautiful chaos around us. As Hispanics, we are loud, dramatic, passionate and proud. You would always see the kids searching every corner of the house for presents, my aunt chasing men out of the kitchen with the rolling pin because they always sneak in to put their hands on the feast before it was ready (or her famous holiday martini), mom trying to find a reluctant dancing partner after finishing her Midori, my sister telling some of her silly holiday jokes and making the family dog dance for us right after a glass of beer and my younger cousins sneaking a few gulps of the eggnog. I guess what I am trying to say is, "My name is Jerry and I am an alcoholic". That warm, fuzzy holiday feeling we all have inside is basically the product of distilled spirits we chug by the gallon in my house. It is the only way we can get through dessert because… yup, you guessed it… it's that darn fruit cake!

It's not like it is inappropriate to drink in excess during the holidays anyway! Christmas itself seems to be the aftermath from the behavior of a drunken person. We go out to nature and cut down trees to bring them inside the house and take the electrical décor and colorful lights to the great outdoors. We hang mistletoe on the ceiling to get some action and hang our socks by the fireplace to be stuffed with candy. How drunk must we appear to people from other countries?!

I sure hope I get better presents than the ones I've gotten in the past. My aunt once gave me a bar of soap, shampoo, towels and hand lotion. It's usually a nice gift when it comes from Bed, Bath and Beyond®; unfortunately, mine had a Holiday Inn® logo on them. Another time she gave me a pink poncho with the picture of a cat on it. Now, let's break this down for a second. First of all, it's a freaking poncho! Who else wears this unless it is the last resource at Disney World® when it rains? Secondly, it's a PINK poncho! I may get a tingling sensation down my pants at the occasional hot dog eating contest and I've been known to shake my groove thang at the clubs, but I am still not THAT gay. Thirdly, it's a pink poncho with the picture of a cat on it! I am terribly allergic to two things: one is cats, and the other is people who post pictures of themselves in (what they think is) a sexy pose on Facebook®. I think I know exactly what to get my aunt this year. I won't tell you because I want it to be a surprise, but you can be sure it will rhyme with the words "fruit" and "cake".

Sometimes I think my Latino 'gente' is delusional. It is usually 80 degrees in most places in Latin America and yet, we still think we can rock the fake snow in a spray can! We have become so Americanized with Santa Claus and the North Pole! We have our villancicos and yet, we turn Jingle Bells into 'Cascabeles' and Silent Night into 'Noche de Paz'.

All joking aside, you want to know what I'm looking forward to? The celebrations! We can turn any holiday into a huge party. What to most seems like a lot of noise and chaos, to us is music and laughter. Not many can dance, cook, and laugh with the passion we employ. The Holidays to us are not even about presents, but about bringing the *familia* together for a few days. No matter how small our homes (or cars) may be, there will ALWAYS be room for someone we love. You can bring a dish to a Latino home and you are welcomed with open arms, no need for expensive bobbles. If you are not Latino, the simple fact that you took the time to learn how to say "Feliz Navidad" with your broken 'gringo-accent' warms our hearts. So, I do hope you enjoy the festivities to the fullest extent: dance 'till you can't walk anymore and eat to your heart's content… just remember to keep the emergency room on speed dial.

"Fruit is good… cake is delicious… Now put them together and you get two pounds of the most horrible thing ever eaten!"

Yay, Christmas!

Ah… Christmas, the season when you buy this year's gifts with next year's money. A time when everybody wants his past forgotten and his "present" remembered. A time to remember that it is no coincidence your family lives so far away and your state of mind is so healthy at the same time. This year, Christmas really felt like a day at the office: You do all the work and the fat guy with the suit gets all the credit.

There is one thing, however, that would have made my Christmas complete…SNOW! It's a shame it never snows in Florida which is where I currently live (unless you count the public bathrooms at the local nightclub). I also didn't get the chance to showcase a live nativity scene, but that wasn't my fault. You know how hard it is nowadays to find three wise men and a virgin?!

I sure got A LOT of fruitcake. Yes, I know I've already brought this up, but it's worth repeating! Fruitcake is like all the evils of the world baked into a cake. Well, guess what everyone is getting from me next year? That's right, bon appétit! And don't you dare return it!

At any rate, now it's time to celebrate the upcoming year and make all kinds of resolutions that we can never follow through. Since the opposite of what I say usually happens every time I make a New Year's Resolution, I'll say the opposite of what I would like to do. For example, "this year I will be fatter, I will not have sex at all, and I will not tell my boss to suck it because I love living in quiet desperation at work." For those of you without a New Year's Resolution, here are some original ones you may want to try:

- I will not insult my friends by giving them fruitcake for Christmas. Have I mentioned how much I hate those things?!
- I will remember that dropping firecrackers inside my friends' pants is not in any way, shape or form considered a good practical joke.
- I will stop buying useless crap like that DVD rewinder I bought for myself last year.
- I will buy a car that I am happy with. Stealing bikes from little girls to get to work is wrong, I see that now.
- I will not bore my boss with stupid excuses not to go to work. I will come up with some new ones instead.
- I will drink less, or I will drink more, whichever is more appropriate.
- I will stop getting into car crashes with hot guys just so I can get their phone numbers.

For the rest of you, I hope you had an amazing Christmas and a prosperous New Year. And remember, good friends don't let other friends drive drunk or buy fruitcakes for other friends.

Cheers!

I saw this adorable couple the other day and they were walking down the streets greeting passersby as they pushed a stroller carrying the most beautiful baby inside. They smiled, waved, talked about their last trip to Europe... Then I stopped for a second and I thought "Damn! I REALLY need a drink!" It's not that I hate people with the cookie-cutter perfect kind of life that I wish I had because I'm a jealous monster. It's simply that, sometimes, I just wish these people…moved…to a…secluded…island in a faraway… planet. Ok, maybe I am a bit jealous. Kidding! I am happy for everyone's happiness. It gives us motivation to better ourselves. Spreading our own happiness and being proud of other people's successes and ours makes this planet much more habitable, in my opinion.

I don't have babies myself, but I used to make up for it by dating lots of drunken guys. You would often catch me saying things like: "Awww, how cute… he's drooling" - "Oh my god, he said my name!" – "Who's your daddy?" – "Uh oh! Somebody made a bubu. Let's go home and clean you up, you piggy".

It amazes me greatly to see the fervor, time and money invested on drinking alcohol in our community. I didn't realize how much I consumed alcohol until someone pointed out to me the way I give directions to people who are lost.

"Oh! I know where that is! You know where Palace Bar is? Well, you make a left there and, when you hit Peter's Liquor Store, make a right and you'll see the home for the elderly you're looking for". - Why do we, as gay men consume more alcohol than anyone else on the planet? What is this void we try to fill, if any? Many are the theories (which also apply to our heterosexual counterparts): drinking facilitates sexual encounters, it allows you to be less shy when talking to people, it releases endorphins needed to forget about your troubles or there are simply not that many outing options other than the bar scene making us all prone to repeat the same experience over and over again. There's nothing wrong with the bars (I myself enjoy the company of my good friend Martin E. Glass) but we, as a community, tend to do this in excess.

Did you know there's a gay cruise, gay bowling nights and gay midnight kayaking? But is that all there is? Have you ever hosted a potluck, game night or theme party at home? What ever happened to the movies, the theater or the beautiful beaches that surround us? Take on a new hobby, invest on a gym membership, read more, indulge in shopping or travelling. Many are the options, and they are just as fun. By all means, have a drink and toast to your life, which can be filled with many resources for fun **and for goodness sake, don't drink like Liza Minelli and you too can avoid having Lindsay Lohan's police records.** If the number of drinks you've had matches the number of times Elizabeth Taylor has been married, you probably had enough.

I understand many are the reasons around us to want to be plastered 24-7: the holidays filled with crazy shoppers, those pesky holiday parties we HAVE to go to, the politics of our nations and our economic situation, the fight for marriage and a safer military life among many other things we try to squeeze in between feuds, breakups, jobs, etc. I know sometimes life may seem like a gigantic evil-ridden monkey just flinging excrement at our faces, but no matter how crappy (pun intended) things may seem, there is always the promise that things happen for a very powerful reason and they will always improve in the end.

Who am I kidding?! Go ahead, have a barrel of beer before things get any worse. I'll be right there next to you in a matter of seconds buying us both the first round of drinks!

"I don't have babies myself, but I used to make up for it by dating lots of drunken guys"

New Year's Resolutions

The time has come for us to fool ourselves into thinking we are going to make all these positive changes in our lives that will be kept all year long. We all want change. We all get that "new year, new me" mentality when we can't even process changing lanes on the road correctly. Some of the most popular New Year Resolutions are the following:

Fitness: We've all been there. We say "I'm going to go on a diet and join a gym and I'm going to look fantastic because I have… Oooh, is that cake?" We actually manage to join the gym, but our weightlifting goes something like this… "One, two, three…Oh my god, I want to die"! – Then a hot guy (or girl) walks by you – "Fourty-eight, fourty-nine, fifty! Nailed it! Grrrrr…"

I actually thought I made a magical connection at the gym once. I walked by this very attractive guy because he was smiling at me while he lifted heavy weights (which is extremely friendly behavior for a gym). I smiled back only to realize he was just grinding his teeth from all that heavy lifting. Awkwaaaaaaaard!

I used to have a trainer but that didn't make much sense to have because a trainer is someone you pay money to so that he makes you go to a place you are already paying for to use the machines that you are already supposed to be using. I'm sure some are great, but mine talked so much about his life that it felt like I was paying him for me to become his free therapist.

Traveling: We all have thought of taking that vacation to go to that place we've always wanted to visit. My life is so uneventful, I fantasize about going to Taco Bell® so I don't have to cook that day. I've always wanted to visit Spain (which happens to be my family's background). I even have the accent to prove it. The more I drink, the thicker this accent gets. I tell my bartender to cut me off if, instead of me ordering libations from him, it sounds like he's talking to the Puss in Boots from Shrek®. "A drink you may serve me, 'bot if I ask yu forrrrr a drrrrink'…call me a cab"!

I'd love to go to Italy also. They have great food. Or maybe the Caribbean. They have amazing dishes. Or perhaps Japan since I love sushi. It seems every country I like is based on the food they have which already tells you I will fail miserably at that first New Year's Eve resolution.

Love: We all want to find love. I can't even find where I left my phone half the time, but it would be nice to have someone by my side to help me look for it. It's hard to find love in our community nowadays, but I remain hopeful. If Donald Trump can marry beautiful women, so can I! All I need is a bank account the size of his ego and for these "women" to have a penis.

You want to make other resolutions that most of us don't consider, but are just as important? You can borrow some of the ones I thought of for myself, spend more time with family, call friends rather than liking their posts on social media or make sure you have more money in your savings account. And why wait for a new year to have resolutions? You want change and improve your life? Do it today!

Baby Talk

And the world gives birth to yet another baby year with the hopes and promises that it will be better than the last. Speaking of babies, my sister just had a baby boy making me an uncle for the third time! I am so glad this crusade is over so that I don't have to hear the stories about chocolate ice cream with sardines cravings or the whole "I was in labor for 600 hours without a pain killer abound!" That little boy sure is cute though; and already acting like a super model! You know… puking after every meal to weigh no more than 13 pounds and staying up for long hours at night. It won't be long before we see him sneaking into the house at 4am with a stamp on his little hand from something that will be called The Crib Nightclub.

I kept asking myself what I could give him for Christmas or her other beautiful kids for that matter. What do you give a baby for the holidays? They are all basically a walking digestive tract with audio, so what do they care? Considering all the terrible outfits my sister makes him wear I figured I'll gift him a pair of sane parents.

"I am so glad this crusade is over so that I donh't ave to hear the stories about chocolate ice cream with sardines cravings"

I Need a Vacation from Vacationing

What a weekend I've had! I told my bartender my Spanish accent gets really strong the more I drink, so he needs to cut me off if he suddenly feels like he's talking to his cleaning lady, Guadalupe, or the Puss in Boots from the movie Shrek®. He forgot all about that, so I left the club with my tab still opened, wearing a shirt that I'm pretty sure I was not wearing on the way in and missing one shoe! So here I am rocking the drunken Cinderella look on my way to the cab. When I say "cab" I mean getting inside a shopping cart being pushed by a homeless guy who happened to be passing by my house that night. I really have to stop drinking!

Well, it looks like vacation time and Holidays are over, and I can tell because there are less tourists and more parking spaces everywhere I go. During the holidays, I get to walk 2 miles to find my parked car because I happen to live where the world comes to vacation, the city of Orlando. Every time the dating app on my phone refreshes, I get hundreds of new faces who are walking around Universal Studios® (which happens to be 7 miles from me) and they are all visiting or asking me to meet them at a hotel nearby. Nothing says "Pretty Woman" like meeting a guy for the first time in his hotel room. I went on a date with a guy once and we had a great time, so I messaged him the next day for a second date. Unfortunately, he was already 1,000 miles away by that time. I wish he told me he didn't live closer to me to avoid the two days that followed after of me crying over his picture and eating a tub of ice cream.

All said and done, I am going to miss my family. We all live miles away from one another. I have family and friends in the Dominican Republic, Puerto Rico, New York, Los Angeles, North Carolina, Texas, Boston, The Netherlands, and London. We are strategically placed in these areas to plan a surprise attack on the world, but you can't tell anybody! Let's keep that between us, OK?

"my Spanish accent gets really strong the more I drink, so he needs to cut me off if he suddenly feels like he's talking to his cleaning lady"

On with the Show

To say that you saw a gay man enjoying a dramatic play in the theater is like saying that you saw a 5-year-old kid enjoying ice cream. What is it about Broadway plays that attract so many gay people? I think tickets to a Broadway show should be part of a welcoming package you get when you come out of the closet along with a gym membership and a $100 gift card to the Banana Republic®. In all seriousness, the theatre world was one of the first to openly talk about the AIDS epidemic in Angels in America and gay identity such as La Cage aux Folles. The theater community has offered an outlet and safe haven to many of us from a very young age. If you would like to see other plays in which gay people are portrayed, do not hesitate to watch Bent, The Boys in the Band, Lilies, The Book of Mormon, Psycho Beach Party, Jeffrey, and fights between my exes and I at home among so many others. So much drama!

I remember growing up as a child, I loved Grease and Mary Poppins. I could never get into Cats though. There was no plot to it! Just a bunch of cats singing about love, midnight, hunger and fleas…I think. Don't quote me on that one. I was not paying much attention. As a young adult I loved Rent, but after a few years, you can't help but to think "shut the f**k up and get a job! If I have to pay rent, why can't you?!" I hear they're re-vamping West Side Story, or as I like to call it "Donald Trump's Hell", as he'd have to get ready to watch illegal immigrants sing for hours about why they want to live in America.

As a gay man, we always try to emulate the theater Divas and they all change according to the generation. First, we had My Fair Lady and Hello Dolly. Then came Wicked and Chicago and now we have…wait, that's right…this generation is not involved in theater as much. Now we have pop stars and cable TV so they're good. I actually started getting back into loving theater thanks to Neil Patrick Harris. Not only is he a good role model as a gay man with his own family and great career, but also incredibly talented as an actor, singer and dancer.

Sometimes I wish my life could be like a big play. I start the day with a song about brushing my teeth as little birds fly through my window and a deer opens the bathroom door with its horns to help me sing the melody. Then, I drive to work, but traffic stops completely because people get out of their vehicles to perform a very enlightening and choreographed dance as the Rush Hour Song plays in the background (which really pisses me off because now I'd be really late for work!)

I love theater because it is a depiction of real human life in a fantastic setting. It fills us with joy, music, and the need to make positive changes in our own lives to try to make them as memorable and beautiful as the ones these characters have. It gives us hope and the promise that, long after curtains go down, they will come up again for us to start a brand-new show in our own lives which will be performed to perfection until we achieve the mental applause we can hear all around us.

I wish you all a fabulous life! Break a leg, guys!

Life is a Party

Well, I started making some positive changes in my life. I decided to free all the sweatshop child laborers I was keeping in my basement, stopped photobombing strangers' wedding photos and released the cure for making solid fecal matter when using the bathroom after a greasy Mexican meal. I know what you are thinking, and the answer is yes, I am a hero.

How was your weekend by the way? Mine was fantastic! I had to learn belly dancing and how to impersonate a woman to lure some spies into my web of lies and steal their secret plans on destruction in American soil. Also, I performed open heart surgery on baby seals and wrestled an 8-foot-tall gorilla as an attempt to save two homeless children lost in the jungle. OK, fine! I did not do any of those things! My life is so boring that finding extra toys in a box of Cracker Jack® makes my day. All I do is go to work, eat cereal bowls four times a day and pleasure myself to underwear commercials. Once again, I know what you're thinking and the answer is also yes, I live a full life.

I was looking for new things that are celebrated in February to find something to talk about and found some interesting things. Aside from Groundhog Day on February 2nd, Valentine's Day on the 14th and this being also Black History Month, I found out we celebrate Umbrella Day, Love Your Pet Day, Eat Ice Cream for Breakfast Day, Canned Foods Day and Spunky Old Broads Day. These are real Holidays! Feel free to look them up. I'm not kidding!

However, I think that when it comes to creating additional holidays for no reason at all, my Hispanic people take the cake. While most of you celebrate Christmas and New Year's Eve, we also have the Three Kings Day in January, The Candelarias and The Old Lady Belen's Day in addition to those. Leave it up to us to find more reasons to overeat, have a party and drink like a fish! Old lady Belen is what we call Santa Clause's wife, and she brins gifts to those who "did not receive a present from Santa on Christmas" because "he forgot". The real reason why she was created was to help mom and dad save some cash by buying toys the day after Christmas when they are not as pricy and on sale. Three Kings Day are the three Wise Men who gifted things to baby Jesus, therefore, we also receive presents on this day. And the Candelarias is the day where we make a fire to burn our used Christmas trees (the real kind of course) and have a party as well around the fire. I'm telling you, whenever you run out of ideas to celebrate anything and need a reason to drink, dance and be merry, give your Latino friends a call. We got you.

Talk about the Three Kings Day! They are also referred to as the Three Wise Men in America. You can tell one of the wise men was wise indeed and did very well for himself because he brought gold to Baby Jesus! But the other two brought him useless stuff that they probably got from the Dollar Store® on the way to the manger.

I can picture the Virgin Mary speaking to them: "So, I see you brought gold. That's so awesome! That is going to help us pay many bills and buy a lot of diapers because babies are expensive! How about you, guys?"

"Well, I have this myrrh...?"

"Uhm… I don't mean to sound ungrateful, but what the hell is myrrh?! It better not be something heavy and solid because I'm about to beat you with it!" - You have to understand the poor woman… receiving guests after a few painful hours of labor without a chance to pretty up for visitors who brought her things she did not understand what they were.

I can imagine the other two Wisemen nodding their heads at him thinking how it was possible they all graduated from the same School of Wisemanship and he couldn't do better for himself. Can you imagine a conversation between his wife and his mother-in-law? She would be telling her daughter - "You could've sold your virginity and services to an Egyptian king or a wiser man, but no! You had to pick the guy at the bar who kept saying he's investing all his stock into myrrh because he swore it was gonna sky-rocket! I can see how smoking all those weird herbs messed with your head! If you weren't burning so much bush, you would've made wiser decisions". Then her daughter would reply "But I love him! I hate you, mother!" - Then she would hop on her vintage Camel GT and gallop away with her Wiseman.

I asked two pastors from a church nearby and they didn't even know what myrrh was! One told me it was some sort of oil and the other one told me it was incense. He probably bought it at Bed, Lake and Not Too Far Away. Get it? They didn't have Bed, Bath & Beyond® in those times. I mean, beds were in existence. I'm assuming people would take baths in the lake and they didn't have anything faster than a horse, so going beyond would've taken months, maybe years.

I'm getting off track here… No surprise there.

He could've gotten him frankincense which would have perfumed Baby Jesus' little booty and make him smell good, but the other one called dibs on it, so the poor guy had to go for something else.

I'm actually feeling inspired to come up with new made-up holidays. We should celebrate the day computers were invented or have a Soup Day or Humor Month or Anti-boredom Month. Would you like to hear something crazy? All of these already exist too! They are actual celebratory days in our calendar! Go ahead, do another Google® search and find out.

Regardless of what you enjoy celebrating, do it safely and in good company. Happy (whatever you are celebrating) day!

New Car, Guys in My Trunk, and a Little Fabric Softener

Today I had a really hard time coming up with things to talk to you guys about...again! This freaking pandemic is driving me insane! My life is as interesting as watching a documentary about introvertive turtles! Latest things that happened to me would be my trip to Sanford in Central Florida or talking to my new friend. I was having a conversation with him, but at times, it's almost impossible to relate to him. He parties a lot, hooks up with different guys every week and is in a perpetual diet which consists of nothing but air, water and a side of guilt. You know the type: they say things like "remember bread"? and talk to you endlessly about 'hot people problems' like - "It's just so hard for me to pick up new clothes because I look good in everything. Ugh! What should I do"?! – I just roll my eyes and say "I know! Don't you hate that? Let's order a pizza". My life is not as adventurous as theirs. Sometimes, when I do the laundry, I don't add fabric softener…on purpose! That's the kind of stuff that makes me feel rebellious and living life dangerously.

Another friend of mine took me to Sanford thinking this place would be more my speed. Have you been there? It seriously felt like I walked out of a time machine a few years back in the past. Every single house gave me that eerie feeling that made me think someone died in there, but the spirit is still guarding the place! Every porch had a rocking chair. That is something you don't even see at many furniture stores anymore. They were only missing the 80-year-old ladies reading the paper outside as they fanned themselves sipping on iced tea and talking about that new metallic flying device that is all the rage. People walked by me, smiled, and wished me a good afternoon, but did not ask me for money! Clearly, I entered the Twilight Zone. I was starting to feel homesick and missed the sound of traffic and rude people, so my buddy slapped me across the face and called me an a**hole. I sighed in relief and thanked him.

I've always been a "city boy" and lived in big cities. Nobody takes long walks down the beach calmly greeting passersby. Most of the walking takes place at the mall and we are watchful of everyone because they all want to steal your money. "Have a nice day" – They would say. "Bitch, I don't know you. Get away from me!" - would be my response until realizing this is the store's cashier being nice to me after I made a purchase.

Another thing that happened to me recently is getting a new car. I was not able to drive for a whole year due to an accident I had. OK, fine! My license was revoked due to drug possession…

…and an extinct breed of monkey I had on the backseat…

…and an illegal alien prostitute I hid in my trunk while he was crossing the border.

But I can drive again, and it feels great to be able to say I am just like everyone else again! I can even vote and drink from the same water fountains as the rest of you too! Wait, I just remember the freaking COVID-19 virus. I don't really go out as much as I did before or even go to the theater to see a movie. I caught myself saying things like "remember going to the movies or the beach?" I cannot believe I said that! When will this end?!

Well, I believe that's it. So, avoid Sanford unless you enjoy good old-fashion values, your mom's cat is your best friend, and you rock to the oldies. Don't forget to always add fabric softener to your laundry and make sure, the next time you hide a prostitute inside the trunk of your car to take home, that he or she is in fact a citizen of this country or at least a legal resident!

Learn from my mistakes! You're welcome!

"remember going to the movies or the beach?" I cannot believe I said that! When will this end?!

Riding the Relation-ship

I once dated the most American guy ever and, the poor innocent corn-fed thing, ended up with the most Latino guy! He's a Southern boy from NC with a thick accent that makes him sound like a Beverly Hillbillies® extra on the show which I actually loved about him. There are many things Latinos have in common with Southerners: we rave about our food, our music and our families. He enjoyed quiet moments sitting on a chair drinking his coffee as he watched the sun rising with the promise of another glorious afternoon. I, on the other hand, have a thick Spanish accent but a lot louder, always in the mood to go dancing every night and enjoy chaotic Latin music as I clean the entire house…the craft of my people. It's no coincidence every cleaning lady and maid on every TV show or movie is called Maria, Rosario or Consuelo. We know how to get things cleaned correctly!

All his friends are always putting crazy ideas in his head. They tell him: "You better watch out for those Latinos and their sex drive. They will cheat on you with a tree simply because it has a hole on it!" He ended up beating me in the race for cheating. I didn't think he would cheat on me. Never say 'never' though. I guess he never heard stories of the many creative consequences that come with messing with Latinos. Like the ones about the Latino guy or girl who slashed the cheater's car's tires or the number of cars keyed after these incidents or the bucket of paint poured on the bastard's car. Why do we always go for the guy's vehicle?! Dating someone of a Hispanic heritage is basically admitting to yourself "I don't care about my car" or "I have amazing car insurance".

They say Latinos do everything faster. When we drive, we are more than likely to have a police car chasing after us thinking we committed a crime when, in reality, we're just trying to make it to the grocery store on our way to watch the game at Carlitos' house. When we dance, in order for any non-Hispanic person to keep up with us, they should…who am I kidding? You won't be able to keep up with that crazy pace. There must be some truth to this statement because my "gringo" ex-boyfriend and I moved in together after 2 weeks of dating (my idea) and I was already proposing ideas for our wedding day! I hoped someday we could get married. Not because I wanted to be somebody's husband but because I wanted him to become the Whitest Mr. Perez anyone has ever seen.

We went through the whole meeting-the-parent's thing. I had to train him first, of course. Dress appropriately and by "appropriately" I mean "overdress" for the occasion. Need help with that? Think to yourself "what would I put on if I was being presented to the Queen of England?" Ta da! Outfit crisis solved. Another one is one they share with just any other parent of any race and that is having good manners. Just because the first words you learn when someone teaches you a new language are curse words does not make it OK for you to use them when trying to impress your future parents-in-law with mentions of your "culo" or how funny it was when your high school buddies would call you "cabrón". Last, but certainly NOT least…your Latina mommy-in-law is the matriarch of every relationship their kids get into so learn to win her acceptance! The most important thing is the Latina mom's cooking. There's this weird connection Latinos have with food. I don't mean to say food is very important to us, but if a serial murderer told us our friends would die one by one unless we stop eating "arroz con pollo" forever (that's rice with chicken), our next move would be to find cheap caskets on eBay®. You MUST rave about her coking and it always helps to ask for seconds. Don't you dare ask her for the ketchup! Might as well shoot her in between the eyes! It's like saying her masterpiece needs fixing and they are already perfect in every way and don't you forget that! She made you fried shrimp and you happen to be allergic to shellfish? Take a Benadryl® and go to town on those suckers!

So, my ex and I had these cute little nicknames for each other. Sometimes we go for types of dipping sauces, so he called me salsa and I called him ranch, other times I am the Rosario to his Karen and also referred to him as my cowboy when he called me "shut up"! You know what? The more I think about it, the less it seems like a cute little nickname for me. It couldn't possibly be. I mean, he couldn't be mad at me because I feel the need to express every thought that goes through my head every minute of every day through texting or conversations face to face, right?! Is it possible for me to continue speaking even when I find myself underwater? Well, yes…as a matter of fact I can! There's no stopping me. I will ear-f**k you for hours!

I hope my new boyfriend and I stay together for a long time (I was serious about the wedding preparations already going in my head). I have designed, planned, and coordinated so many weddings for so many people, but when will I get to be "the bride"?! There are of course benefits from dating a Caucasian guy that go beyond obtaining a higher credit score. I get to feel that sense of entitlement whenever we suck faces. All that White privilege is instantly transferred through my mouth which makes me say things like "you can't talk to me that way because I'm an American and I know my rights!" or "I need to speak to a manager!" Seriously though, I think I find Caucasians attractive because I grew up with a Black-Latino father and many friends with the same gorgeous, tanned skin I have. I've always been attracted to things and people who are different than what I'm used to seeing or interacting with. I can find beauty in things that are dark or things people fear, I prefer rainy days over sunny ones and I like my cereal microwaved & my coffee cold. When I am asked if I have a type when it comes to men, I say (imitating a parrot speaking) "Polly wants a cracker!"

"It's no coincidence every cleaning lady and maid on every TV show or movie is called Maria, Rosario or Consuelo. We know how to get things cleaned correctly!"

To Shave or Not to Shave…That is the Question

My friends invited me to a very fancy party and asked me to groom myself well. I guess I shouldn't have worn those overalls, propeller hat and cowboy boots the last time we hung out. Ok, so I didn't actually wear those. That's why it surprised me when they said that! How many times have you been invited anywhere and had people remind you that you need to look good?! That's when I knew I had a problem. That and the fact that people are always handing me dollar bills when I walk down the street. My "homeless-chic" look should've given me a hint, I guess. I don't care! I'm comfortable. Then again, my comfortable butt may stay single for a while if I don't change a few things. I rather be more Bert and Ernie, not Oscar the grouch®!

I do want to look better. I really do! I mean, I showered today! Leave me alone! (runs away crying).

Okay, I'm back… I know it's not enough to just shower. I just can't get into these modern trends when it comes to male grooming. Let's look closely at some of those, shall we?

The Man Bun… Try to picture an onion stuck to the back of your head and you got the infamous man bun. What in the world would make someone believe this is a good idea to reinforce your masculinity and appetite for appearing virile?! I cannot even count the times I have approached several of these men from behind and said "Excuse me, ma'am". I don't want to see that on a man ever. I mean, that's more of a sexy female librarian thing anyway!

Full Beards… I'm not talking about Goat T's or that 70's porn star mustache or 5 o'clock shadows or not shaving your beard for a month for fundraising purposes. I'm talking about that "lumberjack Paul Bunyan-looking guy sitting at the soup kitchen on his way to the unemployment office" type of look. I have asked people if they are doing the "No Shave November" challenge to raise money for cancer, but no, they're just being gross. Well, perhaps "gross" is too harsh. After all, this is the type of look I search for when wanting to sit on someone's lap before Christmas day. Keep it groomed, conditioned…trimmed even so your lips and jaw line can be distinguished. This way you shall avoid children asking you for toys or the local bluegrass group asking you to join the band. What would you prefer, a screaming 6-year-old or a handsome hunk or sexy lady on your lap? You decide.

Manscaping… Ok, this one is not that unnecessary. I wouldn't want a guy I'm with to feel like he's pleasuring me while getting his teeth flossed at the same time. The only problem is the shaving all over your body while trying very hard not to bleed to death. The positions I get into with that razorblade and small mirror on the floor would make any contortionist jealous! I guess I could also get a body wax, but by that same logic, I could also poke my eye with a fork. That would actually be less painful!

Skin Care… This one is actually important. It's just a hassle trying to remember which lotion goes where. There's one for the face, one for the knees, anti-aging creams, one for the neck…

Excuse me for a second…

(takes a sip of water)

… one for the eyes, one for the legs, one for the elbows and one for the "no no regions". I accidentally covered my torso with the eye cream and now my belly button is able to blink!

Spa Treatments… I am actually glad this is catching on. Who wouldn't want a facial, pedicure, manicure or massage every now and then? This is just one more thing the straight metro-sexual guys took from us "fabulous" men along with dancing well and looking gorgeous. By the way, we want our "OKurrrrrr" and "Byeeeee" phrases back! Now heterosexual women have more men to drool over. You're welcome, ladies! We even made it into a fun game where the girls have to guess if the guys they're looking at are gay, metro-sexual or European. Winner gets to go home with more to cuddle with than a bucket of ice cream, a Meg Ryan movie and a tear-soaked teddy bear.

Anti-Grooming... Yup, this is a trend and I'm not even kidding you about this! Think messy, unwashed hair and bushy, un-plucked eyebrows with a healthy, greasy natural glow. This look is the lazy person's approach to grooming and, it obviously, requires very little effort. I guess the most challenging aspect of this look is being able to get out of bed in the morning. So "trendy"!

Regardless of all the trends we have now, whether you like them or not, it's good to have options and it's good to treat our bodies with the respect they deserve so they are good to us and last us for a long time. Now, if you all excuse me, I have to go apply my cat poop and bleu cheese face mask.

"I do want to look better. I really do! I mean, I showered today! Leave me alone!"

A Life to Remember

Today I decided to get something off my chest… It's this damn 5-pound necklace with the words *Lady Gaga* on it! Excuse me while I put it down… There! That's better. I don't even like Gaga to begin with, so I don't know why I bought it. I mean, maybe she has a couple of songs I like…

Ok, maybe I liked one or two of her albums too…
…which I play every day when I take a shower…
…or listen to in the car…
…or when I'm cooking something…or just always…
…
…
…
…I FREAKING LOVE HER! Necklace is going back on!

But there is something else I'd like to get off my chest if you allow me to get personal with you. In the year 2015, I suffered a terrible car crash, and this caused me to lose my memories. I live with amnesia now and it's horrible because it's not possible for me to remember my whole life before the accident. It's also more difficult to retain new information nowadays. Have you seen 50 First Dates®? It's pretty much the same thing, but it takes me more than 24 hours to forget things. Also, Adam Sandler is not after my booty. I retain only the things I write about. My life today exists just as long as I write it down and go through my notes every month, so I don't forget. I wrote a book about this titled *I Forgot to Remember*. You should get a copy now! Trust me, you'll love it because… well, I wrote it, so it's awesome! Go ahead… I'll wait here until you are done with your purchase…

… … … … … … … …

All Done? Great!

What was I talking about just now?...

Oh yes! Don't you love fish? My friends call me Dory because of that film Finding Dory®. They say I repeat myself a lot and some people had to re-introduce themselves to me several times over a 3-month period because of this amnesia problem that I have. Have I told you about that? Many people tend to reunite with someone they have not seen in a while and say things like "Wow! How have you been?! It's been so long!" When I don't stay in touch with someone for a long time, I say things like "Nice to meet you, I'm Jerry. And your name is?" I am grateful to know people who don't mind playing along so I don't feel bad about it, but I am trying to get better.

Uh… What was I talking about?...

Oh! Don't you love Batman! He's my ultimate favorite hero! Only I didn't know he was because I completely forgot about all the comics, clothing items and memorabilia I collected of this character over the years because of my amnesia. Did I tell you I have amnesia? It happened a few years ago due to a car crash. I was new to everything and didn't get a good grasp of what fiction was compared to reality. Anyway, Once I realized I had a Facebook® account, I looked it over and saw many "get well" messages posted by people who knew about my car accident and many of them had a picture of Batman on those. When I looked inside my closet, none of the clothes were familiar to me and noticed I owned 32 Batman shirts! I was also told I loved working-out, so I asked my sister: "Ok, please be honest. I can handle the truth. Am I this Batman dude? Because, if I am, I'm short a butler and a lot of money right now!" I now own over 68 Batman-themed articles of clothing and, every time I wear them, I take a picture with them to post on my Facebook with captions like "Batman is going to the gym" or "Batman is about to go dancing" because, even though I cannot remember my friends and family members, I know they are watching and I want them to know that "Batman" is still here even if I am a different person today.

What was I saying again?

Oh yeah! I love movies, don't you? I like movies like The Notebook, Memento or The Vow because they have a lot to do with losing your memories. Did I tell you about this accident I had which caused me amnesia? It was a few years ago. Anyway, I love movies. In fact, I always have. However, I believed celebrities looked the way they did when I was a child. Imagine when I saw Harrison Ford today! I thought he was his own father! I had no idea we had lost Whitney Huston and Michael Jackson either. I have been wanting to go to a My Chemical Romance concert, but I am told they are not even relevant anymore. That was my favorite band back in the day. Also, I had to learn how to use a computer, cell phone, drive a car… Just think of me as your great-grandfather who stepped out of a time machine and is now walking in this time trying to absorb all this information about modern technology.

One of my biggest regrets about losing my memories is not having the ability to learn from life's lessons and become a much better and wiser person because of that. Treasure your memories and experiences whether they are good or bad. These will shape you…make you who you are today and what is to become of you tomorrow. Yeah, it may be cool to forget about all those horrible exes you had, but you also forget about your childhood. Having amnesia is not that much of a blessing as others have told me. Yeah, it's great to get away with late rent payments because you just forgot, but you get to also forget about your prom night or college years. I don't really know anyone like me unless they are older and suffering from Alzheimer's Disease, but if you do know someone, feel free to contact me and tell me all about it. I'd love to get in touch with these people!

… … …

What the hell was I talking about?

Right! March is my birthday month so I'm expecting lots of presents from you all! Make them very shiny! Or maybe a movie, or something having to do with Batman. I think I like those, but I'm not sure. Hey, I might have lost a big part of the last 40 years of my life, but I've got 40 more to go and I will make sure they are fantastic. I am certain you're going to have a fantastic life as well! I love you all and, please, <u>remember</u> to be good to one another.

Valentine's Day (A.K.A. One of the Reasons I Drink)

I am a bitter, bitter single man. My hobbies include making brides trip as they walk down the aisle and hold up delicious sandwiches in front of starving passersby so, obviously, you know I'm probably the reason why ejector seats were invented. You may find this hard to believe, but I'm not a big fan of Valentine's Day.

So, what is this about? From a very early age we are taught to believe it is about love and friendship, but then we grow up and realize it's really about showing someone you really care about them...by going broke buying expensive lingerie for your significant other… best friend… your cleaning lady… OK, I need to stop buying people underwear. I'm probably not going to get any gifts myself because I've been a bad boy. Seriously, I am PURE evil! I have been known to use forks at Japanese restaurants… Bad! I've also cut in line at the DMV by pretending I have one week to live and getting my driver's license is my last dying wish… Worse!

Seriously though, it's good we have a day to celebrate love. If you are blessed enough to have a loving "other half", treasure every moment with them. If you have a loving mother, treasure every moment with her. If you have a loving friend, treasure every moment with them. If you have a loving neighbor who keeps going through your garbage and underwear drawers to collect things for the shrine they built in your honor, MOVE NOW! I understand this day is a capitalist's dream come true. Some will argue this day has no historical foundation nor patriotic reason for being celebrated. So why does it exist? We have days for our loved ones already such as birthdays, Mother's Day, Father's Day and anniversaries. So, now I'm entitled to give presents to the same person for a birthday, anniversary, Christmas AND V-day in order to not be branded by my significant other with the "BAD BOYFRIEND" hot branding iron. David Letterman had a very interesting observation about Valentine's Day gifting. He called it "Valentine's Day money-saving tip". It consists of you breaking up with your significant other on February 13th to then get back together on the 15th. Problem solved!

I live in Orlando, Florida so, as you know, I'm only a couple of miles away from magical Disney® castles, beautiful princesses, powerful witches and the most "fabulous-looking" herd of charming princes ever. Not to mention some of the most fun bars I've seen with many tasty libations. Should we consider these to be magic potions because we are in this city? Probably not, but it's the kind of "magical" liquids that give you courage, strength, and can even act as a love potion of sorts. These Disney movies sure gave us the wrong ideas about what a prince charming should act like. Only in Disney movies the broke girl (yet beautiful because it doesn't matter if you're smart or talented as long as you're pretty) will find a rich and handsome man with a great bank account and the worst sense of timing ever! – "I met her at the ball and we danced all night…We must be married at once!"

I am aware that there are many happy endings in our community (aside from the ones taking place in massaging tables), but it is challenging. If anything, take this day to celebrate the people in your life who make it worth living and (most importantly) the love you should have for yourself. Take time to look back at all the wonderful things you have accomplished. Be proud! Then look in the mirror and notice how beautiful you are. Flirt with yourself a little, take yourself to dinner and a movie. Pretend to yawn only as an excuse to outstretch your arm to hold yourself in the dark theater and then invite yourself over for a "nightcap". Once you're alone, go crazy on yourself. Yes! Of course you'll need to wear protection! Hey! you don't know where your hands have been!

You skank!

"I am aware that there are many happy endings in our community (aside from the ones taking place in massaging tables)"

Things I Never Want to Hear Ever Again

These are things I actually have heard (unfortunately):

1. *Does this look weird to you?* (In a public bathroom)
2. *You should get tested.* (After a one-night stand)
3. *Come here and let me examine that rash.* (Referring to me at the veterinarian's office)
4. *Come closer so I can hear you better.* (From a patient who couldn't stop coughing violently while volunteering at the local hospital)
5. *May we come in?* (From a group of Jehovah Witnesses)
6. *This won't hurt a bit.* (At the dentist's office)
7. My full name shouted from my parents' mouths.
8. *Get in the car.* (From a police officer)
9. *We should all jump at the same time.* (While being stuck inside an elevator with a bunch of strangers)
10. *Can you come to the board and solve this math problem?* (In class right after having that erotic fantasy in my head)
11. *Can I help you with something?* (From ANY customer service representative or clerk at EVERY store. If I need your help, I know where to find you)
12. *You can do this! We believe in you!* (At a hotdog eating contest I never signed up for)
13. *We would love it if you came!* (From my friend hosting a Real Housewives® of EVERY state marathon)
14. *Awww! He looks just like you!* (At the zoo's monkey exhibit)
15. *I'm 13 years old.* (In a chat room where you met someone who you thought could be a potential date)
16. *Looks like you're having triplets!* (In a dream where I am giving birth. I'm a man, so I'll let you picture where these babies came out of)
17. *Are you lost?* (In a dream where I appear naked in public)
18. *You are the winner!* (At a Worst Dressed contest)
19. *That's a great idea!* (After I proposed to my friends, we should all go swimming with sharks while wearing Lady Gaga's famous meat outfit. I don't have the best ideas when I drink)
20. *We ran out of toilet paper.* (At the store after eating four burritos during the COVID-19 pandemic)
21. *Reply to this message or I will delete you from Facebook* (Just delete whoever you want, as rude as that is. It's not like it's slowing down your computer. You are just hungry for attention and feel entitled to people's time regardless of how busy they are with their own individual lives!)
22. *Send this message to 100 people or you will have bad luck* (Ugh! I hate chain letters! What's going to happen exactly? Kittens will die? Fine! I'm allergic to cats anyway)

Alternative Titles to Famous Movies

1. Human Centipede = Poop-Guzzling Conga Line
2. Batman = The Vengeful Orphan Millionaire
3. The Blair Witch Project = Ann Coulter Moves to the Woods
4. Cruel Intentions = Life at Any Private Catholic School
5. Finding Nemo = Sushi Menu
6. The Goonies = Worst Babysitter Ever!
7. The Exorcist = Split Pea Soup Dispenser from Hell
8. Titanic = I Bet I Know How This Ends
9. The Hulk = Anger Management
10. Twilight = Necrophilia
11. The Simpsons Movie = A Very Very Very Long Episode
12. Mean Girls = C yoU Next TuesdayS
13. Legally Blonde = Harvard Desperately Needs Funding
14. Gremlins = Muppets
15. The Matrix = Slow Motion Fighting
16. Transformers = Loud Noises
17. Superman = Hot Alien in Spandex
18. James Bond = Over-confident Douchebag Agent 007
19. Maleficent = She's Truly Horny
20. The Avengers = Good Excuse to Make More Action Figures
21. Sharknado = I Paid Money to Watch This?!
22. Brokeback Mountain = Buttsex Mountain
23. Beauty and the Beast = Bestiality and Talking Furniture Hallucinations
24. 101 Dalmatians = Neuter Your Pets!
25. The Princess and the Frog = Took This Long to Have a Black Princess?!
26. The Little Mermaid = The Ungrateful Underwater Brat
27. Cinderella = I Talk to Animals but Thank God I'm Pretty!
28. Boogie Nights = The 2-Hour Penis Shot Wait
29. Step Up = I'm Rich, You're Poor...Let's Dance
30. Showgirls = Lesbian Porn
31. Mulan = The Crossdressing Warrior
32. Avatar = Smurfs on Steroids
33. Splash = I Love Tuna... A Lot
34. Dirty Dancing = Not So Dirty Dancing
35. Star Wars (episodes 1-3) = CGI Wars
36. The Wedding Planner = The Groom Stealer
37. My Weekend with Marilyn = She Wouldn't Remember Who I Am If She Was Alive Today
38. The Witches of Eastwick = Magical Polygamy
39. Memoirs of a Geisha = Pasty Asian Hookers
40. Crouching Tiger Hidden Dragon = We Can Fly, and No One Cares
41. 300 = Hot Half Naked Men Fighting
42. Howard the Duck = My 8-Year-Old Wrote This Script
43. Jaws = My Last Fishing Trip
44. The Omen = I Should've Worn a Condom!

45. Miss Peregrine's Home for Peculiar Children = X-Men The Elementary School Years
46. Amelie = What Did She Say?
47. Edward Scissorhands = Don't Run with Those!
48. The Godfather = The Italian Stereotype
49. Legends of the Fall = How Long is This?!
50. Home Alone = What Not to Do When You're a Parent

The Wizard of Oz. (8-10 p.m., TCM) — Transported to a surreal landscape, a young girl kills the first person she meets and then teams up with three strangers to kill again.
Inquirer Television Writer Lee Winfrey

English to Grindr® Dictionary

There are many dating apps out there. The most popular amongst gay people is Grindr®. These apps are whatever you make of them. I have met two of my best friends on there and have gone on some fun dates. They are also used to facilitate brief sexual encounters with other men in your area. Like I said, it is what you make of it and there is nothing wrong with any of the purposes mentioned before just as long as we are safe and careful. With every dating app, we run the same risks. I noticed there is a lack of etiquette on this and other apps for both gay and heterosexual people. I've always said there should be a book to teach us how to behave properly on these, but there isn't that much to say. I used to be an image consultant for businesses and some people, so I qualified myself for the job. Here are a few things I'd like to share:

When someone says:	What they really mean:
Looking to cuddle	You know we're having sex, right?
I'm of a mixed race or their profile picture is a tree	I'm Black
I'm of an average built with a profile picture of their feet	I'm Overweight
I'm versatile/bottom	I'm a bottom
I'm discreet	Don't tell my boyfriend/wife
I don't parTy that much	I'm high right now
I'm half Italian, a quarter British, 1/3 Puertorrican and 1/4 Spaniard (What are you? A cake recipe?!)	I've never been interesting enough to pass for exotic. By the way, I'm from Florida.
I'm negative on Prep	I have no idea when was the last time I was tested but I don't want you to leave me hanging.
I'm looking for friends	At 3am?! Sure, you are...
Looking for FWB (friends with benefits)	I'll never speak to you again after we have sex
Looking for a gym buddy	We're working out in my bedroom
Send me your picture first (Even though they don't have one up)	Let me see how ugly you are first

I'm not saying all the things mentioned on the "what they really mean" section is negative. I just wished people were more honest about who they are, what they're about and what their intentions really are. Also, I wouldn't choose negative remarks on your profile page. For example, saying things like "I don't know what I'm doing on here" or wasting profile space where you should talk about yourself filled with a list of things you don't want is very negative. Some people start by listing all the things that you should NOT do when you talk to them or advising others to trust no one. These are the profiles that only get the attention from people interested in the way they look and would not pursue anything other than a physical encounter. If you want to be taken seriously, act the part! If you're looking for something casual and don't want to be taken that seriously, that's fine too. Just try to be more approachable.

I can tell something bad happened to these people sexually or got their hearts broken. Don't let anyone have this much power over you because no one has the right to turn people into hateful beings who don't trust others and without love or hope in their hearts. Yes, I used to be a mental health therapist too, <u>but what I'm really saying is</u> "just do as I say!"

"With every dating app, we run the same risks. I noticed there is a lack of etiquette on this and other apps for both gay and heterosexual people"

You know how sometimes you start thinking of horrible things you would rather do other than the one tedious thing you're doing at the moment whether it's work, waiting in line or putting up with annoying people? Well, here are a few I managed to come up with. Can you come up with more?

50 THINGS I'D RATHER DO

1. I would rather get a prostate exam by Captain Hook.
2. I would rather lose my virginity to big foot.
3. I would rather do pushups in the nude with mousetraps underneath my "No No Region".
4. I would rather cover myself in honey and sit naked on a fire ant hill.
5. I would rather get stuck inside an elevator with Jason Voorhees.
6. I would rather play hide & seek with a serial killer or rapist and lose.
7. I would rather practice synchronized swimming inside an active volcano.
8. I would rather use acid as eyedrops.
9. I would rather read an entire dictionary back and forth.
10. I would rather give piggyback rides to every member of The Biggest Loser® TV show before they lose any weight.
11. I would rather play doctor with Jack the Ripper.
12. I would rather play patty cake with Edward Scissorhands.
13. I would rather make out with The Predator.
14. I would rather go on a road trip with the Phelps family.
15. I would rather go hunting with Dick Chaney.
16. I would rather go on a date with an angry tarantula before it had its coffee in the morning.
17. I would rather challenge Kirsten Stewart to a stare contest.
18. I would rather enter an eating contest with Pacman before he had his breakfast.
19. I would rather sit down to explain dumb blonde jokes to an actual dumb blonde.
20. I would rather brush my teeth with a used broom.
21. I would rather get a routine checkup with Dr. Kevorkian.
22. I would rather arm wrestle with a gorilla who's on steroids and determined to win at everything.
23. I would rather use a cactus as a back scratcher.
24. I would rather host a fundraiser for the KKK at the NAACP headquarters.
25. I would rather feed my Gremlin after midnight and then shower with it.
26. I would rather get the medical attention I might need from a professional nurse in Silent Hill.
27. I would rather take a Valium while living on Elm Street.
28. I would rather play frisbee with Xena.
29. I would rather use Crazy Glue® as a substitute for a good conditioner or lip balm.
30. I would rather go to the local lesbian bar and shout "I don't find Ellen DeGeneres that funny"!
31. I would rather eat a dirty sock-flavored Hot Pocket.
32. I would rather develop a smoking habit at the precise moment there's a gas leak in my house.
33. I would rather play croquet with the Queen of Hearts (from Alice in Wonderland) while she's going through "that time of the month".

34. I would rather walk out and get hit by lightning dressed up as the Tin Man and holding a metallic umbrella.
35. I would rather have my mother go through all my conversations on a dating app.
36. I would rather have the shark from Jaws as my swimming instructor.
37. I would rather have a stuttering crack addict sing me the song "My Heart Will Go On" for 10 hours.
38. I would rather dance the Macarena wearing a tube top and a Hawaiian hula skirt in Canada...IN WINTER.
39. I would rather be covered in gasoline while playing Truth or Dare with a pyromaniac.
40. I would rather use sandpaper as toilet paper.
41. I would rather wear red on a date with a bull.
42. I would rather go to a lion petting zoo after they've been starved for a week.
43. I would rather apply eyeliner on myself while riding a roller coaster.
44. I would rather take a cannibalism cooking class.
45. I would rather get a papercut on my wiener.
46. I would rather fall desperately in love with a crocodile.
47. I would rather never eat chocolate just for fun.
48. I would rather kick a sleeping fire-breathing dragon.
49. I would rather have my haircut done with a chainsaw.
50. I would rather listen to the "It's a Small World" ride theme song and nothing else for days.

I would rather go on a date with an angry tarantula before it had its coffee in the morning.

I'm Getting Old!

I've always said that growing old is inevitable but growing up is completely optional. I will always be a kid at heart; however, this "kid" is starting to see gray hairs. I've always felt my whole entire life that my brain never catches up with the rest of my body because I've never felt old and I'm sure many of you will relate to this.

In addition to the gray hairs, I noticed how I am now finding the time to fill out surveys online! I logged into my bank's website to say something nice about the man who helped me open an account there because I thought he was nice. I shopped at Office Depot and the grocery store to then log into their websites (all instructed on my receipts) to fill out a survey and get coupons in return. Then I noticed Barnes & Noble® shopping bags now carry quotes from famous books on them so I had to go on their website to comment on how fun and creative I thought that was.

Oh! And in case that wasn't enough evidence to prove I'm getting old, how about this one...

I am starting to ramble about stupid crap like how I'm getting older because I fill out online surveys and whatnot. Many people get a hint of getting older in many different ways. This is mine... I know I'm getting old because of the quality of life that I dream of having. I used to be a city boy who loved going out to the nightclubs for a drink, dancing and having boisterous conversations and laughs with good friends. I'm not saying there's anything wrong with that, but I am into other things today like quiet evenings at home watching movies with my dog by my side. I'm getting tired.

I wake up each day as the morning sun gently touches the porch embracing me like a tender hug from an old friend who steps in for a visit. I sit down with a cup of coffee as I begin to remember other times the sun touched my face at the beach...and I smile. I go to work and help make the world a better place by providing people with a memorable experience. Then I come back home and pull into the cold driveway at night to be greeted by an overly excited dog who missed me all day.

When I go outside to work on my front yard, I see neighbors getting their kids ready for school and walking their dogs in the morning as I go out of my way to wish them a good day. I take a warm shower in a cold night and cuddle up to a good book or a puzzle game. Seems my comic book and video games days are far gone...sometimes. Then I close my eyes and say a prayer for those who are less fortunate, who don't have a warm bed to rest their heads on. I say a prayer for my family and friends to wish them health, successes and much love. Finally, I say a prayer for myself so that I get to know love once again and share my life with the person who will walk proudly by my side because I'm in his life and nothing could make him as happy as this realization.

You know something? Maybe getting old is not such a bad thing as it reminds me of good old-fashioned values we should all practice at any age. OK, God, go ahead and keep the aging process going. Can I ask for one tiny, tiny, tiny thing in return? Just make sure I stay looking young and beautiful forever. Come on! It's not like I'm asking you for a lot!

The A,B,C's of The Wrong Things at the Wrong Times

I have been known to always make the stupidest mistakes! I am immune to embarrassment and I fear nothing anymore! Let me give you a few examples of how my brilliant mind works:

A) I was once changing the water from my fish tank, so I carefully transported all the fish into a container filled with clean water I had just gotten using a fishing net. As I'm getting ready to drop the third fish, I noticed the other two were floating dead belly up! I dropped the fish I was carrying into the clean water; it swam for a few seconds, its heart stopped and joined the other two floating dead at the top. "What the hell?!" – I asked myself. I tried to grab the dead fish with my hands and noticed it was boiling hot! I must've opened the wrong faucet and filled that bowl with hot water instead of cold! From a closer look, I could even see the steam coming from it!

B) When I moved into my first apartment with my ex, my mother-in-law at the time brought us the most beautiful plant with flowers of different shades of red. She said it was a housewarming present to make the apartment look livelier and more colorful. I promised I would take exceptionally good care of it. I watered it every week and made sure it was close to the window to get sunlight. She called one day to ask how we were doing, and I said we were very happy, and her gift remains as beautiful as ever because of the good care I was giving it. I was so proud of myself because I've always had a black thumb with plants, but I finally succeeded with this one. The last time I had plants to care for was back in the year ninety-ninety-never! She said: "You did what?! Do you know what kind of plant it is? It starts with the letter P". I thought it was a special kind that needed a different type of treatment. So, I started with her guessing game: "Is it a Poinsettia? Petunia? Poison Ivy?!" Her response – "No, Jerry! It's plastic!" – and she began to laugh hysterically at my attempts to water and care so much for a fake plant.

C) A few months later, people at work asked me if I had mints to share. I was carrying a box of mints at the time that I had received at a business expo. It had the name "Siemens"® on the cover, so I thought this was the mint's brand name. Apparently, 'SIEMENS' was one of the companies at that function and were handing out mints as giveaways.

Coworker - "Do you have any mints or gum?"
Me - "I have Siemens" (With my accent, it seemed to them I was offering my semen)
Coworker - "WHAT?!"
Me - "They're really good. Here..."

Then I opened the can to reveal a bunch of white round pieces of mints.

Coworker - "Ewww! What do you do, freeze them?"

Here's the kicker...

Me - "No, that's how they come".

Coworker - "That must be so painful!"
Me - "Uh? Do you want my Siemens or not?"
Coworker - "I think I'll pass".

Ready for one more? Alright, here it is…

D) Last, but unfortunately not least, I received an email from another co-worker who was hosting a Halloween Party/Birthday celebration at his house. I was in the middle of something and I love Halloween, so I didn't read it all the way through. I just RSVP'd right away to get back to work. The day of the event, I rushed to buy him a gift and find a quickly improvised Halloween costume. I didn't have time to do the elaborate costumes I am usually known for wearing (I'm kind of a theatrical perfectionist when it comes to costumes), so I just ripped off some old clothes, put them on and covered my body with fake blood. I rushed over there and, as I entered the house, I realized I was the only one wearing a costume. This girl I used to work with pulled me aside and we hid in the bathroom immediately. "What the hell are you doing?!" – she asked nervously. I asked if I came on the wrong day. "No, didn't you read the e-mail?!" – "Of course I did!"

I lied…

"Did you miss the part about how religious he is and how much he hates Halloween? He has hated this day since he was a kid because his birthday falls on the same day and other kids tormented him with accusations of being a demonic person! We're spending some time with him and sing happy birthday before going to another party where we will be allowed to wear a costume! What are you going to do? He can't see you like that. He'll be so furious!"

Someone knocks on the door. It was him! "Jerry, are you there? I heard you just arrived, but I missed you. You've been in there for a while. Is everything OK?" – My friend and I looked at each other with our eyes opened as wide as possible. I had to think fast! I opened the door and wished him a happy birthday. "What the hell were you two doing in there?! Why are you dressed like that?!"- he says to me with a look of disgust in his eyes. She was speechless, but I started to walk out of there with a pronounced limp and said to him I had just suffered a terrible car accident and she was helping me with my wounds so I wouldn't look so bad when I joined the party. He felt so bad for me he offered to take me to a hospital because I looked pretty bad. In my head I'm thinking 'Damn, I'm good at this makeup thing'. I said not to worry, gave him his gift and said I will just drive myself to the hospital. He insisted, but I just limped out of there and took off. Mike, if you are reading this, I am SO SORRY for not telling you what actually happened! I love you, buddy!

Nightmare TV Ads

I'm not sure what's wrong with me. People have asked me this several times. My answer is that a group of some of the best scientists are working on finding out the reason for my weirdness and they're close to coming up with a solution to my problem. I have been watching TV all day long and watching commercial after commercial. Then it hit me... I can come up with TV commercials too! So, here's my sorry attempt at creating a few of those:

Ketchup: A woman is making hot dogs and preparing a pot of chili on the side which she pours over the hot dogs with melted cheddar cheese.

As she looks into the camera, she says: "I know exactly how to satisfy my hungry man after a hard day of work. Nothing says YUM like some delicious, meaty and zesty chilly from..."

The doorbell rings. - "Oops, that must be my hungry guy". - She opens the door and a man wearing a suit and holding a briefcase kisses her as she welcomes him home. "Hmmm, what smells so good?!" - says the man as he walks into the kitchen and has a little taste of the chili. He spits it out. "Ugh! It has spices in it! You know how much I hate spicy food!"

- "Uhm...I'm sorry. I must've forgotten".
- "Why do you always find new ways to make me angry?"
- "I swear I didn't think it would be that spicy. I thought you'd like something different for a change!"

At this point the man proceeds to unbuckle the belt from his pants and holds it above his head as you would a whip.

- "I work day in and day out trying to provide for you and all I ask is for a little food in return. Is that too much to ask?!"
- "No, of course not! You're right! I'm sorry! Don't hit me! No!!!!!"

The camera pans to a window from the house next door. You can hear the belt slashes, the man yelling and the woman screaming for help from a distance. There's another woman (the neighbor) in this house who looks straight into the camera and says: (sigh) "That Betty is incorrigible" - giggles - "She should've used Heinz Ketchup®". - The neighbor picks up the phone and starts to dial a number while she still speaks into the camera. The woman continues:

"Heinz ketchup is made with tomatoes grown from the best seeds. It's rich, thick, delicious... Nothing tastes better than..." - she now speaks into the phone's receiver - "yes, hello?"

You can hear the voice of a man on the other line uttering the words: "9-1-1, what's your emergency?".

Screen Fades Out to the Heinz Ketchup logo with the tag line: 'Heinz Ketchup... responsible for less black eyes since 1869'

Fabric Softener: A teenage girl is watching TV with her friend until suddenly a huge dog pounces on them after rolling in the mud. It shakes vigorously all over the white couch and area rug! They are now all covered in mud! The girls grab the couch linens, rug and change into clean clothes. As they carry these items into the laundry room one asks the other: "Does this happen often? I realized you didn't get mad or freaked out about all that mess!" Her friend grabs a bottle of Downy Detergent® and then smiles into empty space as she speaks into an imaginary camera saying: "There is no job big or small that Downy can't handle. It will leave these feeling so soft and smelling clean". Her friend looks puzzled. She's trying to figure out who her friend is talking to. She doesn't know what to do. Finally, she decides to humor her friend and looks into the same empty space. She's too freaked out to smile but manages to give a thumbs up directed at nothing in particular.

Suddenly, they both hear someone yelling out "Weeeee!" A small teddy bear is now falling from the ceiling and about to land on their laundry. It sounded something that resembled the voice of a small child. The girl loses it! Her friend (the one looking into the imaginary camera) remains smiling as if she was frozen in time. The girl runs out of that house so fast without looking behind her screaming "BEAR! There's a live bear! Somebody help me!"

Cut to: The same girl who ran out of the house screaming is now speaking to a police officer in a dark room with dim lighting over their heads as she continues to give her testimony from the previous incident. – "That was the last time I saw Becky. It seemed her and her family had been paralyzed by this imaginary camera and I'm pretty sure were completely mauled by this wild beast. My thoughts and prayers are with her family. Damn you, Downy! How many more lives will you claim??!!!"

- Police officer – "But what about the linens? Where they clean?"
- Girl (with a chipper disposition) – "Oh, totally! Thanks, Downy!"

The police officer notices her eyes fixated on an empty space. He looks behind him but sees nothing. "Who are you talking to?" – asks he.

Suddenly, we hear the same "baby voice" as the same bear falls from that ceiling inside the interrogation room.

"Weeeeeee!"

The police officer looks up in terror while he unloads his pistol on the bear as it approaches him rapidly. The cop screams as he shoots – "Nooooooo!"

Cleaning Product: Mom comes home from work and sees her oldest daughter and younger son working on their homework. - "Good lord! Will you look at this mess?!" - says she. Oddly enough everything seems to be cleaned and orderly. Both kids look at each other.

Daughter - "Mom, the house couldn't be cleaner. I don't know what you're talking about".
Son - "Yeah, mom. I know what you're trying to do. I'm going to tell dad if you do this again. I mean it".

Mom - "Tell dad what, sweetie? That apparently I'm the only one who cares the house isn't spotless?"

Mom grabs a bottle of Mr. Clean® and suddenly a small cyclone of aromatic fragrances wooshes from the bottle revealing a muscular-bald man with white clothing so tight it leaves very little to the imagination.

Mr. Clean – (Using a very heroic tone) "There is no dirt Mr. Clean wouldn't be able to..."

Mom – "Mr. Clean! Thank goodness you're here. I was wondering if you could help me with...something in the bedroom...the shower! The shower is just SO dirty!"

Both kids roll their eyes.

Mr. Clean – "Say no more! Lead the way!"

As mom directs him to the bedroom, she touches his forearms - "Ooh, someone's been working out". They enter the bedroom and lock the door behind them.

Son - "This is crap! I'm calling dad right freaking now!"

TAGLINE: "Mr. Clean will be sure absolutely EVERYTHING is clean before you come home".

Dating App: We see a man and a woman sitting by themselves in the hospital's waiting area. Their eyes meet. The man shows her the cast he is wearing on his leg as if to say "this is why I'm here" as he shrugs his shoulders. She shows him the cast on her left arm and shrugs as well.

They both laugh.

He shows her a cut on his elbow and she shows her a small scratch on her neck. They both laugh again.

She then proceeds to show him a rash with boils on her shoulder. He's not laughing. In fact, he is starting to look concerned. That does not let her stop there. She removes her dentures to reveal the gapped fangs-like teeth she was hiding behind that beautiful smile. She continues to remove the other arm which was easily detachable.

He has a frightened look on his face, but she still smiles.

There's more. She removes her hair to show she is completely bald, removes her glass eye and finally removes her shoes and socks to reveal eight toes on each foot. By the time she stands up straight again to share more smiles with her new friend, she realizes he is not there anymore and probably left her alone after all these revelations. She shrugs her shoulders as if to say "oh, well" and takes out her phone to look at a Dating App called Love Connections. She looks absolutely beautiful in her profile photo!

TAGLINE: "Love Connections, a place where you can be whoever you want to be and attract as many unsuspecting victims as you want".

I've been told I'm odd, or weird (which is the same thing) my entire life. Fitting in has never been something I was able to master. It still isn't. As an adult, the terminology has changed to "random". I find acts of randomness extremely funny for some reason. For once, I'd love to see a commercial with a scene starting with a guy angrily slamming a Barbie doll ® on the floor as he screams "I don't care. I never loved you anyway!". His friend walks in and says something like: "What's the matter Bob? Still stressed out about your car insurance? The rest of the commercial is about an insurance company his friend is recommending. Just have things starting in an odd fashion for no reason or say things at random for no reason at all. It breaks tension and it makes people laugh.

I had a friend of mine who would say the name of the first thing he sees as we are talking on the phone. I pick up the phone and say "hello". His response is "doorknob" or "sirloin" or "fruit basket" or "cats". I start laughing because I know exactly who it is and now, we are talking for an hour even though I didn't feel like talking to anyone that day. I had a boss who would send us e-mails with a random subject line once. It read PENIS. "What?!" – is what everybody would say before opening it almost immediately. The subject of the email began with the sentence "I know you hate reading my messages in the morning, so I needed to spark your interest. And now that I have your attention, etc. etc. etc.

Let me tell you, there was no e-mail we didn't read from him after that one in the hopes we ran into something funny. It never happened again though. He never really had a good sense of humor unfortunately. Also, he was fired after being accused of 3rd degree murder. Yeah, I think that could've been the reason why we stopped getting e-mails from him. Kidding! Just being my old weird random self.

"I'm not sure what's wrong with me. People have asked me this several times. My answer is that a group of some of the best scientists are working on finding out the reason for my weirdness and they're close to coming up with a solution to my problem"

Buy Coffee If You Dare

I went to a nearby coffee shop the other day. I won't tell you the name of the establishment, but it rhymes with "Bar Box". I was having a rough morning. So, I decided to calm my nerves with a little treat. A teensy little vanilla latte with cream, No big deal, right? Except for the fact that I'm a moron and don't visit these types of joints often. "Size?" – asks the barista. I explained I wanted a medium size cup. He sighs as I am being harshly redirected to the display of cup sizes in a different language (I'm pretty sure it was Italian). Why can't they figure out whatever the word for "medium" is in their caffeine ridden world on my behalf?!

Dick Rudesky (I just made up that name to go with his personality), says I actually want a "tall" cup. A "short" is "small, venti is large, tall is medium and I'm guessing "up" is "down"? Am I in Wonderland?! I was beginning to wonder if I was being a victim of one of those hidden camera shows and Dick Rudesky was just an actor. You know "Dick" is short for "Richard", right? Just making sure you know I'm trying to make this a wholesome anecdote. Anyway, the barista bastard boy rolls his eyes at me once again, as he clarifies: "DO YOU WANT THAT MADE WITH HALF & HALF". Dick drones and drools a wet spot on his protective mask through which he can only mumble through. Yes, Dick wants me to confirm the drink I ordered is still the same drink I ordered 15 seconds prior. Unfortunately, I don't speak Rude Trollish and couldn't hear whatever noises his face was making on the first shouting marathon.

"What was that?" - I inquired since I couldn't understand what he was trying to say.

DICK rolls his eyes again, elevates the volume of his voice to approximately 8 million, and asks his question again.

"First of all, don't yell at me. Secondly, are you seriously asking me if I want my beverage which name UNDOUBDEDLY means 'made with half and half' since I said I wanted cream in it?!" – This was my response.

Then, he ACTUALLY utters the phrase "I HATE THIS! OMG! I HATE MY LIFE!".

To which I replied: "That's so funny. We are so alike it's freaking me out! You're not going to believe this, but I hate your life too, Dick! You are a prick!

"Sir, your drink is going to be down at the end." – he says.

"Oh, and by the way, my name is Jerry. Don't you dare spell my name wrong as you are all very famous for doing because I'm going to go ballistic! Today is not the day for that kind of crap!" – was my parting message.

He scoffs and says nothing. I go to the area he instructed me to go to. He takes a sharpie to write on the cup. Oh Lord! Smoke is coming out of my ears as I'm picturing all kinds of horrible things he is writing on it to piss me off more. I'm even making a fist as he walks towards me with the cup.

He drops it in front of me. I grab it to read if it has my name misspelled on it on purpose since he "forgot" to say my name, so I could identify this delivery was my own. I turn the cup around slowly… Oh my God! Here we go…

He wrote: I'M SORRY, JERRY.

What?! No! You're supposed to be the bad guy of this story and now I'm the one who feels like a total dick! (You are what you eat, I guess). I said to him: "I'm sorry too. You're alright. Thank you for my coffee". He doesn't work there anymore. If you happen to be reading this, whatever your name is, I wish you good luck in your endeavors. I really do.

"Dick drones and drools a wet spot on his mask through which he can only mumble through"

Anger Management

Wow! I just had a major realization and I hope it helps many of you who find yourselves in the same position as me. Have you ever heard others say that gay people tend to snap a lot? It's either that or people saying how they love our witty and sharp attitude. "Lesbians are so angry and gay guys are so bitchy all the time"! - is what I often hear.

On a personal note, I have been told I have anger management problems my whole life. I've yelled a lot, broken things, fought people... I am not easy to control. I attempted to study humor and became a comedic writer and fun individual. That was a blessing in disguise, but also a trigger for more anger. It became my defense mechanism. Turns out clowns never get a day off. You are not allowed to have a bad day when people associate you with laughter. You could have been robbed, lost a job or a pet and the world will always come to you saying "make me laugh because I had a bad day". No one is there to make YOU laugh.

I remember feeling so drained after finishing a comedic piece for the magazine I worked for or making someone's day better. It's like you run out of "funny juice" and then go home alone left with nothing for yourself to enjoy and I am not the best company for myself, to be honest. I cried so many times for no reason at all! There's a reason why every comedian throughout history has suffered from alcoholism, suicidal thoughts, drug abuse and anger management problems.

I have been taking a very good look at my life lately and, being in my mother's home surrounded by so many pictures, triggered a lot of emotions in me. I remember spending years after years hiding in the proverbial closet pretending to be someone I am not for fear of not being loved by anyone anymore or going to "hell" after I'm dead. While everybody else was enjoying their youth, I spent it constantly worrying and looking over my shoulder with a secret to protect.

Then I am told that there is a risk of being infected with many diseases I haven't even heard of if I exercise my right to be loved by the person I want to love while my heterosexual counterparts were just making sure not to get pregnant. So, every three months for the rest of my life I have to go to a clinic and have my blood tested and wait anxiously for the results every single time. It's like being nominated for a very prestigious award about something you've very good at, but hoping you don't get it. It's nerve-wrecking! I still took pregnancy tests every now and then just for the thrill of peeing on a stick and to practice waiting anxiously for a test result.

Because I am a man, I was cursed with the same brain that every other man in this world has. We tend to be very visual creatures. I am instinctive sometimes, but other times, the male hormones take over and act on impulse whether it is a negative or a positive response. So, for this reason, I tend to be a very visual creature and try not to ask for directions when I'm lost. For this same reason, we are judged by others based on appearances. We are under the watchful eye of the world, so we have to look the part: we have to look presentable and show everybody that we can live successful happy lives being who we are. We are judged within our own peers because I need to look attractive or "hot" enough to be loved and accepted by other people who ironically, have felt rejection in their lives and should know better than to inflict this pain onto others.

I've experienced discrimination, abuse (physical and mental), seen other gay people murdered for being who they are and been invisible to many. I'm always fighting! Fighting against society and family (who are supposed to be your support system). When you are being discriminated against because of the color of your skin, you can always turn to your family because you're all the same and can support each other. When you are gay, you can't exactly always count on these people for support and other men in your community will judge you if you don't look like a centerfold model.

I look in the mirror every morning and say to myself that I have to be funny, go through severe workout routines to look my best, and protect myself even from people who I want to be close to. I fight anger every day of my life because of these things! It feels as if I should have a lawyer and hitman on speed dial! From a very early age I learned that, because I'm a short person, the chances of me winning a physical fight would be close to being nonexistent. This is why I had to make others feel they would lose if they were ever to have an altercation with me. Therefore, I had to teach myself how to say the right things with a sharp tongue and loud or aggressive tone of voice and drive the biggest SUV and always be in a position of power at work. If I were a dog breed, I would definitely be a Chihuahua...the loudest small dog in the animal kingdom (not to mention, Hispanic). I have been nicknamed after anything that is short, tanned and has unmatched bravery such as Scrappy Doo or Jerry the mouse! This is where I got my nickname, Jerry. The name I was given at birth was my grandfathers'...Gerardo & José. Living in America made me realize that many people cannot roll the letter "R" to make the sound my name requires, so I am Jerry, now and forever.

You think I have an issue with anger? I'm actually surprised I haven't killed anyone yet! I have to say I am proud of myself for having gone through life just taking it all in (the unfaithful boyfriends, discrimination, memory loss, lies, deception, failed attempts at building a career or a home, having your property stolen a few times, overcoming the death of a loved one, fighting addiction, etc).

Yes, we ALL go through a lot in our lives. I am simply referring to my own experiences and the fact that I have gone through all these and still face the world with a smile on my face and a silly joke to tell others trying to make their days brighter. Next time you hear me say a joke, say 'thank you' because you know it takes a lot from me to want to get up in the morning with a positive disposition. Next time someone snaps at you, ask them if they're OK instead of feeding into it. This is the way we should be with others all around us. There is a lot we don't know behind every word and every face we encounter in our lives.

Let's try not to judge others and imagine what it would be like to walk a mile in their shoes before we open our mouth and close our hearts to others. Hopefully, they wear nice shoes that will complement my outfits.

We never know when we will take our last breath on this earth, so be sure to live your lives with pride and create memories that will leave a smile on other people's faces every time you are being remembered or talked about. Be sure to leave this world in a better condition you found it in. The purpose of life is to be happy and make others happy in the process. Take care of yourselves and each other!

The Vaccine is Here!

They found a vaccine to combat the COVID-19 virus! I cannot believe I have to write about this, but here we go. This segment is not to push any agenda or force anyone to do anything. I cannot believe I'm saying this, but I'm doing this to defend myself from attacks I received online.

I have been attacked online because of my postings on social media about the vaccine and COVID-19. I always make sure I am well-informed, and I like to share this information with everyone I know. I've gotten many negative responses, for some reason! To doubt the advances that we have achieved is an insult to those who have put their lives on the line so that we can finally be at this stage in our lives which signifies the beginning of the end of this horrible virus. It's an insult to people like my mother (who is a doctor) and, if you insult her, you are DIRECTLY insulting me. I wouldn't mess with me if I were you. I usually walk around with very sharp pencils in my pocket. Just a fact… not a threat… maybe. Take it as you will.

These are some of the comments I've received and, quite frankly, pissed me off:

"I saw your post and I'm sick and tired of hearing about this virus"

Do you want to know what I'm sick and tired of? People dying over this. Also, restrooms at gas stations. Those are just gross!

"This vaccine is just a scam to make money from innocent victims"

There are people out there who are announcing they have a vaccine for a cheaper price online. Do not fall for these! Do not take this out on the doctors who have the answers we are looking for. Unless I'm the one selling the vaccine online. Yeah… I'm pretty reliable. Come on! Daddy needs a new jacket!

"It's too new, so let those stupid guinea pigs die before I get vaccinated"

Those "stupid guinea pigs" happen to be doctors, political leaders and first responders (police, firemen, etc.), not to mention people over the age of 65 including my mother. We would be lost without them. Why would they vaccinate these people if it was such a risk? I invite you to listen to your common sense. Be very careful with the words you choose before you address me, please. My mother is not a stupid guinea pig, and neither are those who volunteered months ago at the risk of losing their lives so that we can have this today. Plus, guinea pigs are cute as hell, so shut up!

"How could you possibly know anything? You are no biologist or a doctor"

You're right, I'm not. But that doesn't make me not a smart individual and caring person as I've always been. I have dedicated every second of my life trying to be informed to help others around me. Have you? So? You're not going to answer me? Uh?! Well?!

Oh, right... This is a book you are reading and there is no possible way you can answer me. And now I am just talking to myself.

Great! Moving on...

"I have a cousin who studied medicine and tells me that we should wait"

Do you want to throw titles at me? In that case the therapists, family doctors, pediatricians, surgeons, dentists and even veterinarians in my family should have no credibility? I'm not an expert even though I studied psychology in college as a minor and became a case manager and mental health therapist for seven years. Medicine runs through our veins in my family and so does the search for new information every day. Incidentally, I've always been told by many doctors and nurses that I have very good veins. I'm starting to think that's a pick-up line at hospitals.

"People have died over this. You're just killing more people with the things you say"

There have been six deaths since this started due to pre-existing medical conditions these patients had. No one has died because of the vaccinations. If you fear your pre-existing medical conditions could affect you negatively, consult your doctor. I can't say this enough! If I wanted to kill someone, I wouldn't suggest they get vaccinated! I would just push them down a cliff or dress them up as ice cream cones before abandoning them at a fat camp in Egypt... in summer!

You don't have to be vaccinated if you don't want to, but I consider that to be a bit selfish because I'm going to make sure I stay safe and it would be unfair to be around people who are not immune to this and still want to be around me. Just think about that for a second. TALK TO YOUR DOCTOR and stay informed, do the right things for your body (treat it with respect: no drugs, numerous sexual partners, bad eating habits and lack of exercise, etc.) and make the right decisions.

We are in the 21st-century and we have been able to develop vaccines and cures for diseases better than we did in the last century. How is it possible that no one made a fuss about Viagra or drugs to prevent HIV infections which I take myself. Granted, there were side effects the first week I took them, but that is not the case anymore. And Viagra? Come on! I guess it's more important for people to get their one-eyed monsters hard rather than to protect their families and friends from something that could kill them. You tell me.

We have to trust the people that have been fighting for us for a very long time risking their lives, time with their families and money so that we can be safe. And we should also observe and keep in our prayers those who have fallen because of this horrible virus.

The virus is new, fortunately it is composed of things we have dealt with before which made it easier to find a temporary solution or the beginning of the end for this virus as it has been called. Once the vaccine hits the muscle, it sends a message to our blood cells to create antibodies that will protect us from this virus. It is not a cure or a virus to attack another virus. It has no viral properties. It will not go into our DNA, so it won't change anything that defines us as a person.

Because it is a new vaccine it may take a while to cater to everyone in the world. We are producing as much as possible to make sure we all receive this. This is why the phases were developed. Not only is it protecting people who are on the front lines first and foremost, but it buys us time to produce more of this vaccine globally. This is not a matter of someone being better than others, rich versus poor, etc. This is a virus, so the first people we want safe are those who are battling it. Then we want people who are at a higher risk of dying from this so they can have immunity to this and so forth.

.5 out of 10 people experienced side effects similar to the symptoms of the virus itself, but they went away seven days after being vaccinated. We still don't know if you can be infected with the virus once the vaccine has been applied when coming in direct contact with people infected, but these are extreme forms of transmission (sexually or having someone coughing or sneezing DIRECTLY at your face which is SO rude!). This is why the use of masks is still encouraged but not enforced for people who already received the vaccine. I'm not sure how people are going to differentiate the two, but that's what I know so far.

We are also encouraging people to avoid large gatherings and try to celebrate the holidays and other festivities with close relatives instead of a bunch of friends, coworkers, etc. We don't really know who might be infected so we have to live with the mentality that anybody can infect us.

Eating fish, fruits, fibers and not consuming too many calories helps us get our bodies ready for this treatment. Doing cardio for 30 minutes to an hour can help your body become stronger and increase the chances of us staying healthy and be able to not have any side effects (or make these minimal) when being vaccinated. Avoid trans fats and carbohydrates as much as possible.

Be safe, encourage others to be safe. Take care of each other and take care of yourselves. We are all ONE human race…brothers and sisters in this world fighting against the same things and trying to achieve the same goals. Love yourselves and one another!

Fear and ignorance have been the cause of many deaths throughout history, not vaccines. If you agree or disagree with me, I'd rather you have open discussions about this with others. We are together in this. We are a community, and we should talk about this as such.

"To doubt the advances that we have achieved is an insult to those who have put their lives on the line"

DC Comics®

The title doesn't refer to the amazing comic book company we've all come to love over the years. The title of this piece stands for all the horribly laughable acts some of the people who live in Washington have been responsible for.

What in the world is happening in D.C.! I feel like Alice watching news of Wonderland on TV wondering how it is possible for the Mad Hatter to still have supporters! I am referring to Donald Trump, of course. This man is the biggest embarrassment in the United States history! His resume includes and it's sadly not limited to: separating foreign parents from their children "Holocaust-style", using offensive language to refer to women, the LGBT community and people from other countries. Also suspending cancer research funds to go towards funding a war he was trying to initiate, ruining the political and financial relationships we had with other countries, responsible for 10 years of tax evasion, inciting people to use violence against others, and using social media (Twitter®) to discuss private and/or political matters like a 15-year old girl with a lot of free time on her hands would do! Now "sore loser" is to be added to the list because he keeps stating he lost the election because some of the ballots on his favor were stolen! He encourages his supporters to "defend their country" at all cost inciting the violent and crazy acts his supporters are known for.

There has been no evidence of foul play, yet he swears he should've won the presidential election. And now we see people protesting violently as they hold their confederate, Russian (a communist government), and other flags with threatening messages attached to them. People, someone who received support and funding from the KKK is obviously not fit to run this democratic country! Even some republicans have "abandoned the ship" and do not support the actions of this man. We are, once again, the laughingstock of the world! Thanks a lot, Trump for creating hatred and separatism amongst Americans one more time. Way to make an exit, you racist, homophobic and misogynistic piece of human excrement!

Whoa! I'm sorry about that. I don't know where that came from! I usually keep my feelings bottled up inside until they become $3,000 worth of psychiatric sessions.

Democrats and Republicans alike, PLEASE stay safe. If you're in the DC area, stay away from this chaotic experience! If you are gay, Black, Hispanic, transgendered, foreign, disabled mentally or physically, in the military or a woman THINK before you vote again! See if your decision will go in favor of someone who cares about all of us or his own personal agenda and the glory of only some!

I Rather be Blue Than Yellow

I am a walking contradiction: I hate apples, but love apple pie. I like cleaning, but hate washing windows or dishes. I love sunflowers, but hate the color yellow. Blue is peaceful like water or the sky, red demands our attention (which is why it's used a lot in advertisements) and it's the color of passion and love, fire, blood (life), and then yellow is there yelling out: ==HEY! I'M YELLOW. LOOK AT ME EVERYBODY! I'M SO BRIGHT AND SHINY!== (sings) ==THEY CALL ME MELLOW YELLOW!== (I am making this statement using captions and changing the text to that color to illustrate how annoying it really is). Just making a point. This is why some people prefer it as highlighter colors to pinpoint the importance of some sentences because it's the only color that is there saying ==PAY ATTENTION TO ME! LOVE ME, DAMN IT! LOVE MEEEEEEEEE!==

I picked up the bible and started reading through some of its passages hoping I could find things in there to cheer me up. Before you start praising me for being such a good boy, I should tell you that I read it simply because the power went out and I couldn't finish watching the movie that was playing before this happened. Ugh! Life is hard! Anyway, I was using a highlighter to mark some of the passages I found more inspiring until my mother saw me and screamed to high heaven: "What are you doing desecrating that book like that?!" Apparently, it's a sin to use a highlighter on the bible? So, I guess I'm going to hell. You know something I found very interesting? The bible speaks of Jesus Christ when he was being announced, then his birth, miracles he performed as a small child, and then BOOM! He is a man recruiting guys to be a part of his gang and yadda, yadda, yadda… I ask you… ==where is teenage Jesus?!== (I'm highlighting this in case He's watching and needs me to make this easier to find). There are no talks of the embarrassing acne or his first kiss, prom night or being shoved inside a locker because he was such a goodie two shoes!

Sometimes I picture that maybe this is omitted because he was kind of a snob in high school? I know, I know…I'm already going to hell for using a highlighter on my mom's bible, but hear me out. If you were a teenager AND the son of God, wouldn't you use that power to show off and make some friends as you raise up to the top of the popularity chain? I mean, all he had to do was look up and say: "Daddy! They're being really mean to me!". A minute later… ALA-KAZHAM! The bullies get eaten by a group of rabid camels! Or picture Him driving up with a bunch of his buds to a drive-thru window at the nearest fast-food place. The voice on the speaker would've said "I'm sorry, Jesus. We stopped serving breakfast at 10am" – "Oh really?" he would've responded as he snapped his fingers. – "You're right sir. I apologize. We never stop serving breakfast no matter what time it is and please accept these free strawberry milkshakes for you and your friends". Then everybody would've gone "woo hoo! Jesus! Jesus! Jesus!"

Yay! The power is back on! Ok, back to watching more movies and take a break from desecrating my religion. I'm sure He did it just so I stop talking about Him revealing the truth of those wonderful teenage years. ==Thanks, Jesus!==

The Extra Mile

The world has advanced due to people who make a difference, and making a difference puts you on the map. People will consider the things you do as being too much, and it will be for a while until people start considering this is the way things should've been for years. Without these actions, we would've never had a Marilyn Monroe, Queen Elizabeth or Charles Chaplin. To many, these people were slutty, a blasphemous simple woman and immature. Guess what? Sometimes who you are is exactly what you need to create this change. Follow your dreams no mater how crazy or silly others might think they are. They are only trying to bring you down because you are already above them! Dare to be different and always be a little extra even if others think you're to much.

Allow me to share a famous quote which explains this concept magnificently:

"At 211 degrees water is hot. At 212 degrees, it boils and, with boiling water, comes steam… and with steam, you can power a train. One degree! Applying one extra degree of temperature to water means the difference between something that is simply very hot and something that generates enough force to power a machine".

I have been fortunate enough to live through several heart-warming experiences when I worked as a server for a restaurant. I have been asked to pose in photos with guests simply because I brought a balloon to their tables or performed a card trick because it was someone's birthday. A little girl shared a drawing she made for me to remember them by because I offered to place a napkin on her doll to act as a bib. These little actions made their day. They were already happy with our food, ambiance and the fact that I always made sure they never run out of water. It's that little extra joke or action that turned these experiences into memorable moments.

On a personal note: I live with amnesia caused by a car crash I suffered years ago. For this reason, I am not promised I will remember moments in my life today or what my life before that accident was like. I value memories more than anything in the world and, if I can give someone else (with the capacity to remember moments in their lives) a great memory to take home with them, I will do whatever it takes to make sure this happens. Not to mention, it will always encourage our guests to come back and form long-lasting friendships with others.

"I have been fortunate enough to live through several heart-warming experiences"

The Angry Chiwawa

Stupidity is not generational. I often hear people blaming the previous and newer generations for what's wrong with the world when the only problem we've always had is that this planet is overpopulated by humans and humans make mistakes. I once made the mistake of turning to drug use. Talk about meeting the wrong kinds of people! It seems people have been praying to the gods to give them something that could grant them the powers of hallucination, so they see themselves as beautiful, funny and active individuals. That's when the Greek god Fuckedupitus invented crack. Enter meth heads, jockstrap gatherings and hallucinations of "shadow people" (those won't do anything to you because they don't exist. The people who will cause you real problems are the ones that you bring to your house as they steal from you and start fights for no reason). For participating in these gatherings, I've been told I'm going to hell. Yet, one more reason why I'm being sent there.

If I was to speak to a religious fanatic and ask what kind of people are in hell, they'll say it's people like me. If you ask them what kind of people are in heaven, they'll say it's people like them. I don't know about you, but hell is starting to look pretty awesome to me and they really need to work on their threats.

I've always been a short guy with a short fuse (an angry little Chiwawa), but I much rather fight people for what's right. I have been called a superhero because I'm always trying to "save the world". One time, I heard mom screaming "NO! You can't do that!". I called her name from the first floor in her house, but received no answer. I immediately stood up to save the day and, let's face it, the possibility of me winning a physical battle is -300. But there I went anyway. Fanfare sounds! Turns out, mom was just instructing my grandmother on how to apply insulin on herself in case she needs a dose and no one's around. She is hard of hearing and was doing it incorrectly, so mom had to scream instructions at her.

That didn't stop me from rushing into her bedroom and kicking the door open as I'm holding a knife in a stabbing position over my head. I scared the crap out of them!

Did I save the day? … Not really. Will I always try to save the day anyway in the future? …

Absolutely!

"I've always been a short guy with a short fuse"

Give Me a Break!

It's not easy being a clown. You have to be funny all the time whether you like it or not. Our job is to make the whole world happy and we are not allowed to have a bad day. We don't have the luxury of being human... to cry, to feel, to remember...

We go to the same bars you go to every now and then to drink your sorrows away and then there's always that one guy that will come out to us and say "make me laugh, clown"! So now I have to put on my mask or face paint and put my sorrows away to make sure they get a chance to do the same with theirs.

They'll laugh, go home with a smile on their faces and wake up energized to face a new day. During their lunch break, they'll approach their colleagues and talk about that funny thing he heard from me at the bar. My words will resonate in others and make more people smile.

On the other end....

That same night at the bar ends with me going home alone and emotionally drained because I gave all of me to that stranger who needed a laugh. I cry myself to sleep and try to build myself back up thanking God, once again, I was not able to build enough courage to grab that gun in my drawer and end my life once and for all.

Don't turn your back of facades. A smile could be hiding a lot of pain and anger. To my fellow clowns of the world who may not be as "happy", please get help. The world needs clowns, but clowns need the world. It's no coincidence most comedians are alcoholics, suicidal, drug addicts, depressed or temperamental. Humor is a great way to deal with life's troubles, but it could be a weapon. It can be a life force or a taxing weight on our shoulders if not used properly or when needed. Find the telephone number of your nearest suicide prevention center. They also have hotlines if needed. Please, take care of yourselves! I cannot stress that enough.

People complain too much about too many things. It takes value away from the simple things that are created with the best intentions.

There is always a comedian that we find annoying, offensive or talking nonsense about things he or she obviously doesn't understand. His views are different from the majority so he's obviously wrong.

Or one of those stupid online tests that people post on social media every day that are supposed to reveal something about your personality. How stupid must you be to consider those as being accurate? Which character from the TV show Friends® am I? According to this test scores, I'm a Rachel! It seems I am driven, emotional and will make my dreams come true if I work really hard and apply myself even when others don't think I have what it takes... Yeah right!

Or the slow people we have to wait on while they are cleaning something that we cannot wait to use such as a bathroom facility or a restaurant table.

Or that damn dog that is always jumping on me making me always go to work covered in hair. But if we take some time to look at things from a different perspective, we will then learn to appreciate the things we consider to be a nuisance sometimes. Maybe that comedian is making a point to keep a certain issue relevant and not forgotten just as long as it's being talked about in a negative or positive light. Not to mention the countless hours they spend coming up with material that could brighten your day. Maybe he or she overcomes insecurity issues, self-esteem barriers and fear of rejection every day to allow him/herself to set worries aside to be able to make you laugh so that you can forget about your problems.

Maybe those online tests are there to give people at random a few words of encouragement that could serve as the necessary fire that will ignite the will to go on and face any obstacles they may have with confidence.

Maybe those annoying people cleaning that table or restroom you're about to use, comply with their minimum wage duties so that you don't have to put up with an unsanitary environment.

Maybe that dog hair all over your clothes could be saying more than "I am an unclean person" or meaning that your pet needs to be disciplined. Maybe these can be worn as badges of honor because you are loved, and someone is always excited to see you come home.

Think about it. Is the world really the way you see it or is there room for improvement in the way you see the world?

"Don't turn your back of facades. A smile could be hiding a lot of pain and anger"

If I Could Turn Back Time

As I type the title of this entry, I can't help but picture Cher sitting on a huge cannon wearing leather and fishnet stockings singing "If I Could Turn back Time". And I just revealed how old I am. Great. Now I'm really wishing I can turn back time by hopping in a sickening DeLorean.

Wow! A DeLorean?! Really?! Man! I have got to stop making references about my age! I am often troubled with thoughts of wanting to turn back time which could be easily resolved if I thought before I spoke. There are so many people I didn't have to push down the stairs if I apologized and took the higher road! Ugh! That darn higher road! I hate heights, but this one is a necessity at times. But what I'm really referring to is turning back time to bask on the simple things that made us happy when we were kids. There is a lot we can learn from nature such as paternal instincts and there is a lot we could learn from children.

We used to get along with kids from different races, gender and physical disabilities until we learned about racism and discrimination. Look at kids today. You put them all together in a room and a sense of curiosity will awaken in them. Pushing others aside because they are different from us is something we all learn from adults when we are kids. Ironically, these are the role models we should look up to for guidance.

Maybe one day, you can take some chalk and draw a game of hopscotch on the floor. See which passersby play as they go about their daily walk. Or walk up to a complete stranger and tap them on the shoulder as you say "you're it"! See if they follow through with this and find another to infect with this silly game until we have a whole group of strangers playing! Imagine going to a staff meeting starting with your boss saying "I spy with my little eye…" as a warming or ice breaker exercise. Maybe you can play Hide & Seek with your spouse when he or she comes home from work. Use a jump rope to add to your cardio and indulge in a FREE HUGS campaign with you and your friends.

Think outside the box and dare to play more. You will make the kid inside of you very happy! Go ahead! I super triple double dare you!

"Think outside the box and dare to play more"

LEarn

Cooking, Crafts & Things

Cooking Recipes:

The Chocolate Coma

Holy mother of God almighty! I created a dessert that is so decadent, I raved about it for days! It's so good, it'll make you want to bathe in it and use it as soap as you try not to eat yourself! It's my new chocolate obsession (after Jason Derulo, of course). It's so good, you will sell everything you own just to have a little piece in exchange! It'll make you want to pinch your nipples as you eat it! That reminds me, do not consume in the presence of children and do not hesitate to head straight to the hospital right after. Your nips will need reconstructive surgery!

Ingredients:

Chocolate milk

Chocolate cereal (I used Cocoa Pebbles®)

Chocolate ice cream (the kind that has brownies in it)

Your favorite chocolate (I used Hershey's Kisses®)

Nutella® (this one is not required but makes it even more decadent!)

Directions:

1. Put all the ingredients (except for the Nutella) in a bowl and mix well with a large spoon.
2. Place bowl in the microwave for 2 minutes.
3. Mix it all together using a potato masher or use a blender.
4. Place mix inside a baking sheet.
5. Place container in the freezer for 4 hours.
6. Take it out of the freezer and use a metallic spatula or knife to cut it in squares (as big or small as you want them to be).
7. Smear a little Nutella on each piece with a butter knife.
8. Enjoy and, for the love of God, try not to have an orgasm!

Unicorn Poop Cookies

Ingredients

- ½ cup of butter, softened
- ½ cup of shortening
- 3 ½ tablespoons of cream cheese, softened
- 1 cup of sugar
- ½ teaspoon of salt
- 1 egg
- ½ teaspoon of almond extract
- 2 cups of all-purpose flour
- 24 drops of assorted food coloring, or as desired
- **Sprinkles!**

Directions

- Combine butter, shortening, and cream cheese in a large bowl. Beat using an electric mixer until smooth. Add sugar and salt; beat until combined. Beat in egg and almond extract until well mixed. Gradually add flour, blending until dough is combined.
- Form dough into a ball with your hands. Stretch into a log shape and divide into 6 portions, or 1 per each color you plan to use.
- Center 1 portion of dough on a large piece of plastic wrap. Poke a well into the center with your thumb. Add 3 drops of food coloring into the well; fold dough over the coloring. Seal with the plastic wrap and knead the food coloring into the dough. Add more food coloring if needed. Tint each remaining dough ball with a different color.
- Chill the tinted dough in the refrigerator for about 1 hour.
- Preheat the oven to 375 degrees F (190 degrees C). Grease a baking sheet.
- Divide each tinted dough ball into 8 equal pieces. Refrigerating the rest while you work, roll 1 piece out into a 6-inch rope over a waxed paper-lined or lightly floured surface. Repeat with the remaining dough pieces, stacking 1 rope of each color into a pile to make 8 multicolored piles.
- Gently press the ropes of 1 pile together and use your hands to roll the large multicolored 'rope' until round and smooth. Lengthen to 10 or 12 inches if desired. Cut in half. Use your hands to gently twist and roll both ends of each half in different directions. Use your imagination to coil rope pieces into the shape of unicorn poop. Repeat with remaining dough.
- Press silver candy or sprinkles into the dough pieces. Place cookies on prepared baking sheet.
- Bake in the preheated oven until cookies are set and bottoms are light brown, 8 to 10 minutes; they will not spread very far. Cool on a wire rack.

Easy Crème Brûlée

(Incidentally, this is also the nickname of a "very popular" French girl I knew in college)

Ingredients

- 5 large egg yolks
- 3/4 cup (150g) granulated sugar, divided
- 3 cups (720ml) heavy cream or heavy whipping cream
- 1/2 teaspoon espresso powder (optional but recommended)
- 1/4 teaspoon salt

1 and 1/2 teaspoons pure vanilla extract

Directions

- Preheat oven to 325°F (163°C).
- Whisk the egg yolks and 1/2 cup (100g) of granulated sugar

together. Set aside. (At this point or before you temper the egg yolks in the next step, bring a small kettle or pot of water to a boil. You'll need hot water to pour into the baking sheet for the water bath.)

- Heat the heavy cream, espresso powder, and salt together in

a medium saucepan over medium heat. As soon as it begins to simmer, remove from heat. Stir in the vanilla extract. Remove about 1/2 cup of warm heavy cream and, in a slow and steady stream, whisk into the egg yolks. Keep those egg yolks moving so they don't scramble. In a slow and steady stream, pour and whisk the egg yolk mixture into the warm heavy cream.

- Place ramekins in a large baking pan. If you don't have 1

pan large enough, bake them in a couple pans. Divide custard between each ramekin, filling to the top. Carefully fill the pan with about a 1/2 inch of the hot water. The baking pan will be hot so use an oven mitt to carefully transfer the pan to the oven.

- Bake until the edges are set and centers are a little giggly.

The time depends on the depth of your ramekins.

Our ramekins are 1-inch and the custard takes 35 minutes.

Begin checking them at 30 minutes.

For a more accurate sign, they're done when an instant read thermometer registers 170°F (77°C).

• Remove pan from the oven and, using an oven mitt, remove the ramekins from the pan. Place on a wire rack to cool for at least 1 hour. Place in the refrigerator, loosely covered, and chill for at least 4 hours and up to 2 days before topping.

• Using the remaining granulated sugar, sprinkle a thin layer all over the surface of the chilled custards. Caramelize the sugar with a kitchen torch and serve immediately or store in the refrigerator for up to 1 hour before serving. (Caramelized topping is best enjoyed right away.)

HAM AND CHEESE CROISSANT CASSEROLE

Ingredients

5-6 large croissants slightly dry
1/2 lbs ham cubed
7 large eggs
1/2 cup 2% milk
1 tsp garlic powder
1/4 tsp ground mustard
1/2 tsp salt
1/2 tsp black pepper
1 cup shredded cheddar
1 cup shredded mozzarella
1-2 tbsp green onion sliced

Directions

1. Pre-heat oven to 350 degrees F.
2. Prep all ingredients: Cut croissants into ~1 inch cubes. Cube ham. Slice green onions.
3. Grease a 9 x 13 inch rectangular casserole dish. Add cubed croissants to dish.
4. In a large bowl, combine and whisk eggs, milk, garlic powder, ground mustard, salt and pepper.
5. Add egg mixture to casserole dish filled with croissants. When pouring, making sure to pour all over and onto as much of the croissants as possible. This is to make sure we get most of the croissants moist.
6. Add ham, shredded cheddar and shredded mozzarella and spread them evenly.
7. Bake in the oven covered for 20 minutes. Uncover, and bake for another 20 minutes.
8. Remove from oven. Garnish with green onions. Serve and enjoy!

Cook time: 40 minutes

Pavlova Recipe

Ingredients

For Pavlova:

- 6 large egg whites room temperature
- 1.5 cups granulated sugar
- 2 tsp corn starch
- 1/2 Tbsp **lemon juice**
- 1/2 Tbsp **vanilla extract**

For Cream:

1 1/2 cups heavy whipping cream (very cold)
2 tbsp granulated sugar

For Topping/Decor:

4-5 cups fresh fruit blueberries, kiwi, raspberries, sliced strawberries, etc.
15 Mint leaves for garnish, optional

Directions

How to Make Pavlova:

Preheat the Oven to 225° F. Line a large baking sheet with

parchment paper. Using your stand mixer, beat 6 egg whites on high speed 1 min until soft peaks form. With the mixer on, gradually add 1 1/2 cups sugar and beat 10 min on high speed, or until stiff peaks form. It will be smooth and glossy.

Use a spatula to quickly fold in 1/2 Tbsp lemon juice and 1/2 Tbsp

vanilla extract, then fold in 2 tsp corn starch and mix until well blended.

Pipe meringue into 3 to 3 1/2 inches wide nests onto the

parchment paper using a Wilton 1M Tip. Indent the center with a spoon to allow room for cream. Bake at 225° for 1 hr and 15 min then turn the oven off and without opening the door, let meringue in the hot oven another 30 min. Outsides will be dry and crisp to the tap and very pale cream-colored and insides will still be marshmallow soft.

Transfer the pavlova with the parchment paper onto the counter or a cookie rack and allow it to cool to room temp. Once cool, you can top them with whipped cream and fruit or store in an airtight container for 3-5 days at room temperature (in a low humidity place).

How to Make Frosting and Assemble Pavlovas:

Beat cold whipping cream with 2 Tbsp sugar in the cold bowl for 2 to 2 1/2 minutes or until whipped and spreadable.

Pipe frosting onto the pavlova and top with fresh fruit.

White Chicken Chili

Servings: 6 servings

Prep: 15 minutes

Cook: 35 minutes

Ready in: 50 minutes

Ingredients

- 1 tbsp olive oil
- 1 small yellow onion, diced
- 2 cloves garlic, finely minced
- 2 (14.5 oz) cans low-sodium chicken broth
- 1 (7 oz) can diced green chilies
- 1 1/2 tsp cumin
- 1/2 tsp paprika
- 1/2 tsp dried oregano
- 1/2 tsp ground coriander
- 1/4 tsp cayenne pepper
- salt and freshly ground black pepper to taste
- 1 (8 oz) pkg Neufchatel cheese (aka light cream cheese), cut into small cubes
- 1 1/4 cup frozen or fresh corn
- 2 (15 oz) cans cannellini beans
- 2 1/2 cups shredded cooked rotisserie or left-over chicken*
- 1 Tbsp fresh lime juice
- 2 Tbsp chopped fresh cilantro, plus more for serving
- Tortilla chips or strips, Monterrey jack cheese, sliced avocado for serving (optional)

Directions

Heat olive oil in a 6-quart enameled Dutch oven over medium-high heat. Add onion and sauté 4 minutes. Add garlic and sauté 30 seconds longer.

Add chicken broth, green chilies, cumin, paprika, oregano, coriander, cayenne pepper and season with salt and pepper to taste. Bring mixture just to a boil then reduce heat to medium-low and simmer 15 minutes.

Drain and rinse beans in a fine mesh strainer or colander then measure out 1 cup. Set whole beans aside, transfer 1 cup beans to a food processor along with 1/4 cup broth from soup, puree until nearly smooth.

Add Neufchatel cheese to soup along with corn, whole beans and pureed beans and stir well. Simmer 5 - 10 minutes longer.

Stir in chicken, fresh lime juice and cilantro. Serve with Monterrey Jack cheese, more cilantro, avocado slices and tortilla chips if desired.

For more delicious recipes, cooking classes and catering to private events, visit U Can Cook at Ucancookcelebration.com in Celebration, FL or visit Facebook.com/ucancookfl

Ice Cubes

Ice sandwich, ice juice and ice soup

Ingredients

- Water
- Ice Cube Tray

Directions

- Take Ice Cube Trays out of the freezer
- Fill each tray with 2 cups of water
- Place trays back inside the freezer
- Remove trays from freezer after 4 to 6 hours and enjoy as you wish

Chocolate Bunnies

Ingredients

- Bunnies
- Chocolate Cream
- Cherries

Directions

- Place bunnies inside a deep box. This way they won't be able to jump off to their freedom.
- Use chocolate cream to pour over their little heads and bodies. Feel free to use gloves to make sure the chocolate is smeared well all over them. Make sure it's EVERYEHERE. bunnies love that!
- Place a cherry on top of their heads and avoid opening your door to members of P.E.T.A. (By the way, these are great for Valentine's day!)

Punishment Dinner

Ingredients

- Bread
- Water

Directions

- Just serve as is. This homage to prison food is great for kids who misbehave and spouses who just don't get it. For a more miserable effect and really stick it to them, place these items in plastic disposable containers.

Niños Envueltos or Wrapped Up Children

(courtesy of my dear aunt Tuti)

> NOTE: No child was harmed during the preparation of this dish! Except for my neighbors' kids. I can finally get some sleep around here! Thank you, Jesus!

INGREDIENTS

No kids! (allegedly)
Cabbage
Rice
Malaguetta (about 8 to 10 leaves)
Garlic
Onion (half)
Tomato paste (16 oz.)
Salt (2 tbs.)
Ground beef (1 lb.)
Extra virgin olive oil
8 Lemons

Directions

Mash the malaguetta leaves and salt together. I used a pilón (mortar) to get the job done. Great for smashing things. Just ask Hulk's latino cousin.

You will need to use your hands to execute these steps for better results!

1. Take these ingredients and add to the uncooked rice. Mix them well together.
2. Mash the garlic, onion and add to the uncooked ground beef. Mix all of these well together.
3. Squeeze lemon juice and add tomato paste onto these and knit with your hands again.
4. Add 1 cup of olive oil and keep knitting.
5. Boil cabbage in salted water after cutting the bottom (root) off and dismantle its leaves as it softens.
6. Take each cabbage leaf and place some of the mixture with the beef and rice on it.
7. Roll each leaf with its contents and place aside.
8. Take all rolled-up cabbage leaves with the rest of ingredients inside of them and boil in salted water (on high) for 1 hour. Be sure to add a bit of that virgin oil inside the water. Make sure the pot you use to cook is deep enough to fit all these items inside of it.
9. Pour more water if you notice it evaporates before the hour has passed.

Chilly Cheese Dogs

INGREDIENTS

Hotdogs
Cheese (your favorite brand)
Hotdog Buns
Ice cubes

Directions

1. Place hotdogs and cheese in freezer for a week.
2. after a whole week of explaining to your family why you keep those in there for so long, remove the items.
3. break hotdogs apart with a mallet or smash on the floor after your spouse has confessed how much he/she spent on that new outfit using the money you saved on your joint bank account without discussing it with you first.
4. place each hotdog inside a hotdog bun.
5. break each cheese square into three 1/inch rectangles and place on top of frozen meat.
6. Feel free to place some ice cubes around the meat to make it "chillier".
7. Serve on a plate (not disposable ones) and give to your worst enemy or your spouse for spending that much money on an outfit without telling you.

How to Make Paper Roses

Once I was coordinating a wedding for a friend of mine and she lost her bouquet minutes before walking down the aisle! I asked all vendors at the venue we were at to grant me 30 minutes before they begin with the ceremony. I asked the staff at the hotel we were in to gift me some papers from their office. I grabbed all bridesmaids and gave them all small stacks of paper, scissors and glue. That turned into an improvised arts & crafts class as I instructed them how to make paper flowers. We all did so wonderfully that no guest could tell they weren't real flowers until having a closer look! I also ended up changing the tire of their getaway limo. I know what you're thinking and I agree with you… they should've paid me half a million dollars after all that crap I went through! Here is how these beautiful flowers were made…

Step 1: The Setup

You will need paper (8 ½ x 11), clear glue, scissors. Cut 1 inch off the top of this page and then cut four squares of the same size.

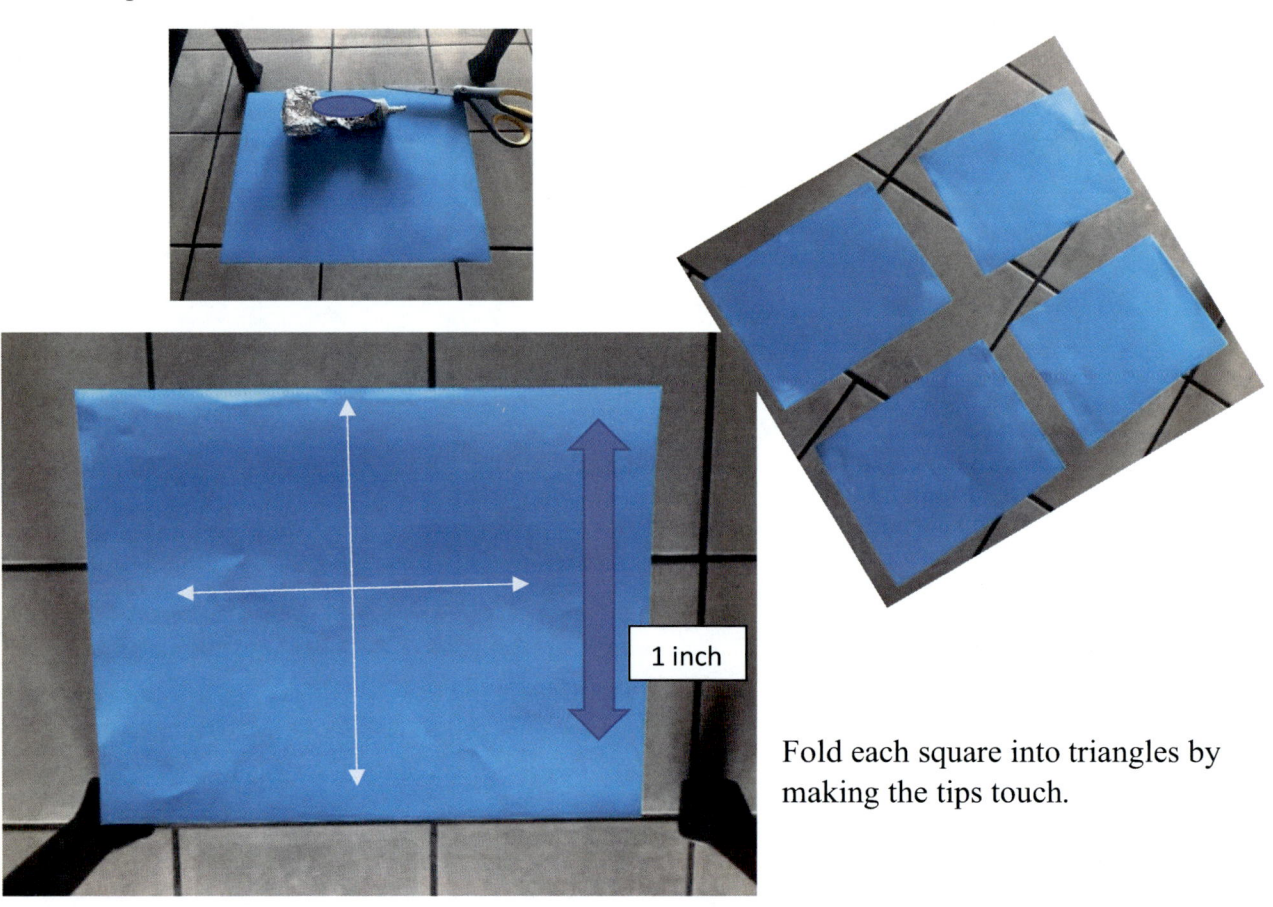

Fold each square into triangles by making the tips touch.

94

Then do it again…

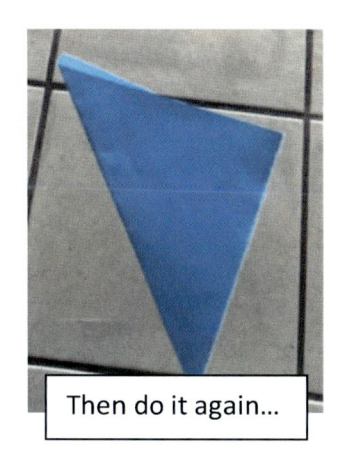

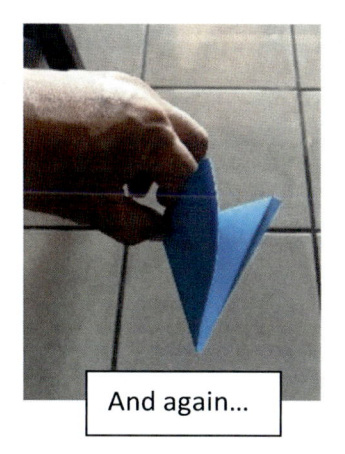

And again…

And again until the end of times.

Congratulations! You have successfully completed Step 1! Have a celebratory glass of wine!

Step 2: You Made the Cut!

Take a quarter and use this to draw a semi-circle on top of the folding. It has to be the size of a quarter. USA! USA! USA! LOL. Man! What was in that wine! Anyway, cut the semi circle drawn and then unford to reveal 4 flower-shaped… wait a minute… why do I only have 2? Anyway, make sure YOU end up with 4.

95

You will then cut each flower as so: one petal off the first one, then two petals (or foldings) off the second one, then three petals off the next one and so on.

Holy mother of Edward-freaking-scissorhands! I just cut myself and boy does that hurt! Oh yeah, make sure you don't cut yourself. They are not kidding when they say "don't run with scissors". They mean it! Now I have to run to the wine cabinet to numb the pain. Anyway… are we having fun or what?!

Weeeee! Flowers!

STEP 3: FOLD IT, GLUE IT, LOVE IT, DRINK IT…

Hey guys! Nice to see you again! It's been so long! LOL. I'm kidding! I know you haven't stopped reading this part of the book. Man! I am drrrrunk, biatches! LOL. OK, this is where sh*t gets real… Now, you'll need to fold the one single petal you cut earlier and then glue it closed. Use the scissors to fold the petals and use a rapid motion to…ugh! What's the word I'm looking for here? Scrape it? It should force the paper (petals) to fold at the top. Then use glue to connect the flowers again after yo savagely cut through them. Lord! I overdid it with the glue and now it's everywhere! This paper moves so much on my fingers!

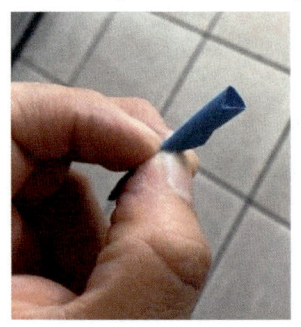

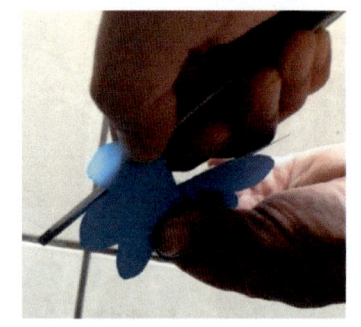

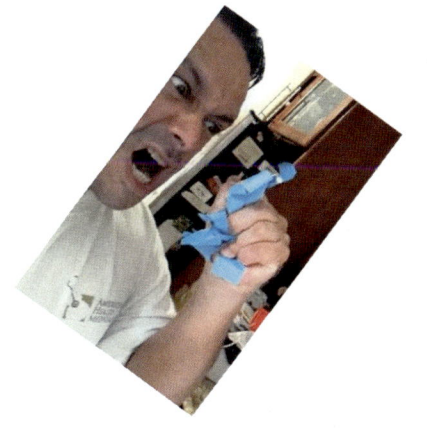

It's like I need two freaking people to finish the job! You know what I need? Some more wine. Yeah, that'll do it.

OK, let's get this crap over with! Now, that you have your stuf folded and glued together, you're going to glue the flowers you cut earlier inside one another from biggest to smallest. Five petals go inside the one with six petals. Four petals go inside the one with five petals, and so on. Piece of cake, right? The last one you'll add to the group is the single rolled up petal in the center.

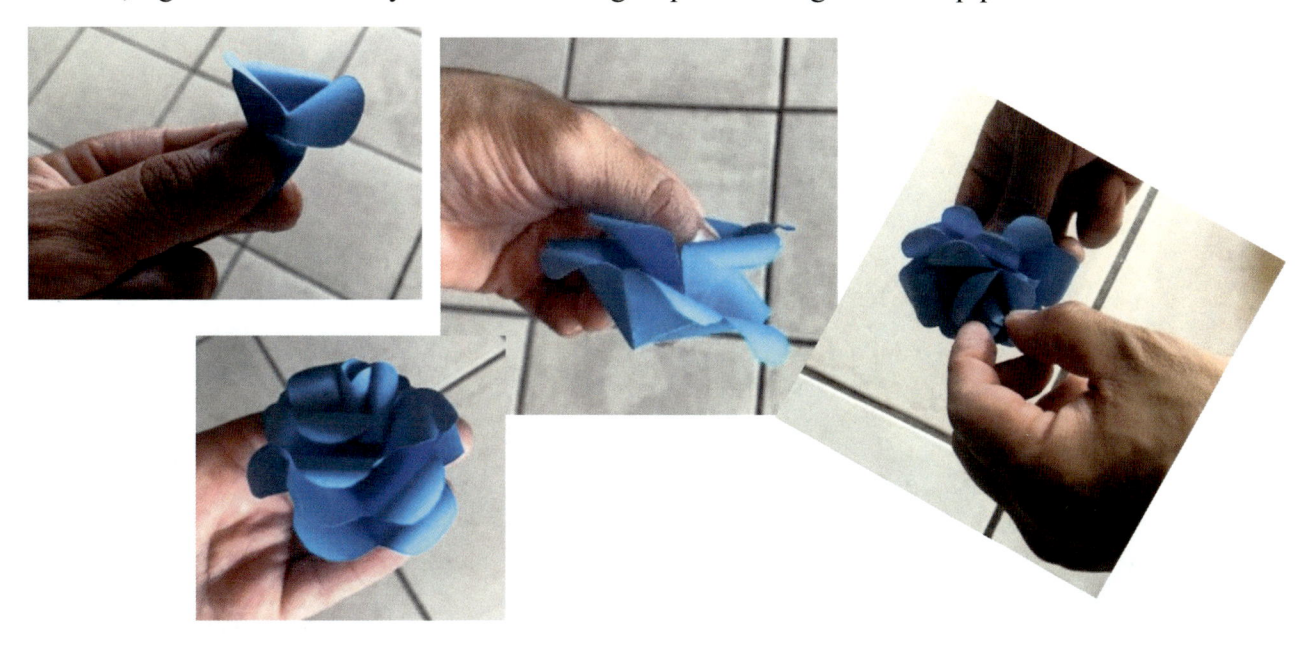

Now, do the same for the other three… wait a second. Where are the other stupid flowers? I don't get it! They were here just a minute ago! Arrrrrgh!

Why do you have to be so stupid and forgetful, Jerry?! What in the world is wrong with you?! My college professors were right about me, I'll never be able to acomplish anything in life. I can't do anything right! ANYTHING! Somebody, please, love meeeee!

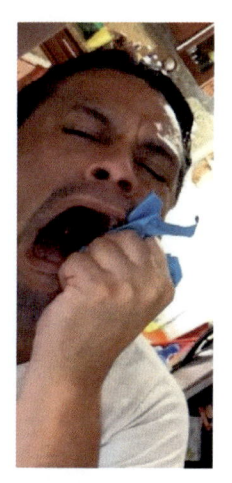

Well, if you still have any willpower in you, feel free to do the same thing to make other roses of any color you want. Wasn't that fun? Now, if you all excuse me, I'm going to finish the rest of this wine and head over to the local florist to buy me some more of those thingies, but live ones. God already did a wonderful job making flowers, so why am I wasting time playing God? Why are YOU playing God? You got something to prove? Uh? OK, love you… byeeeeeeeee!

98

I saw The Sign

I ♥ U Love

A as in "Ahhhh! Chocolate!"

B as in "Baby wants some chocolate"

C as in "CHOCOLATE" (what else would it be for?!)

D as in "Dude, where's my chocolate bar?"

E as in "Ewww! You don't like chocolate?"

F as in "Fudge brownies are better than sex"

G as in "God, grant me the serenity to accept there's chocolate I cannot eat...because a day only has 24 hours!"

H as in "How did you forget to bring me chocolate?"

I as in "Ideally, I would have chocolate for breakfast, lunch and dinner"

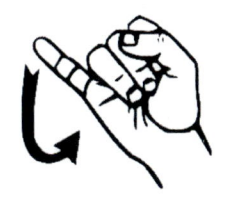

J as in "Just shove that chocolate bar in my mouth now!"

K as in "Kids are so easy to steal chocolate from!"

L as in "Let them eat (chocolate) cake" – is what Marie Antoinette really meant to say.

M as in "Mom, can I have chocolate for my birthday?"

N as in "No, I don't think I am THAT obsessed with chocolate"

O as in "Oh, yeah...spread that melted chocolate all over that ice cream, baby!"

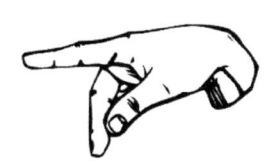

P as in "Pardon me, sir...are you going to eat that chocolate popsicle?"

Q as in "Quick! Put the chocolate inside the bag!"

R as in "Raisins are a poor substitute for chocolate chips in a cookie"

S as in "Silence! Bring forth more chocolate!"

T as in "Tears ran down my face as I saw there was no more chocolate left"

U as in "Under no circumstance will I ever quit eating chocolate"

V as in "Vanilla mixed with chocolate means less room for chocolate"

W as in "Who ate my chocolate ice cream?! Prepare to die!"

X as in "Xylophone rehearsal ended with a round of chocolate shakes" is"

Y as in "You need to be very quiet when I'm enjoying my chocolate"

Z as in "Zebras will never know how good chocolate

Party Ideas

I am a certified Event & Wedding Coordinator, so I have multiple ideas for all types of parties, themes, designs and décor. I cannot share all of these with you for legal reasons. However, I have hosted private parties in my house including Murder Mystery Dinner Parties where I had the guests enjoy a great meal, play a fictional character (dress up as such as well), Oscar Night Parties, Game Nights (board or video games) and birthdays. I want to share two with you that seem to have been most successful and I hope they help you create amazing memories.

Anti-Valentine's Day Party

My friends and I were talking about how fed up we were with the propaganda the entire world gives to this occasion. We were all single, so we never felt like we could be a part of this. I kept reminding them this day was about LOVE. It doesn't have to be just for couples because there is also the love we have for our families, coworkers and friends.

A week before Valentine's Day, I mailed them invitations with the letters S.A.D. (Singles Awareness Day) and a picture of a wounded Cupid. They were encouraged to wear red or hints of the same color in their clothes. The ceiling was covered with hanging hearts and other red décor and the walls had many hearts with sarcastic messages about love written on them such as:

- Love: A dirty trick life plays on you to preserve the continuation of the species.
- Love is what happens to two people who don't know each other well yet.
- The good thing about masturbation is that you don't really have to dress up for it.
- I haven't spoken to my wife in years… I didn't want to interrupt her.
- Behind every successful man stands a very surprised mother-in-law.
- Love… a temporary insanity curable by marriage.
- The last thing I think about on Valentine's Day is a toddler flying towards me with a weapon!

The décor may be similar to that used on Valentine's Day such as hearts (not the ones we see in biology class) and flowers.

Food

You can serve any type of food you would like as this party theme doesn't require a specific kind. Maybe serve food items that are red or pink in color or use food coloring for this effect. Just make sure the buffet area has a sign that reads "LOVE BITES" and the bar has another sign that reads: "LOVE SUCKS" to point out these are the areas to grab a BITE to eat or SUCK (from a straw) and drink the many libations available to the public with the double entendre that goes with the "anti-love" theme. I chose to toast to this day and to thank all who attended with champagne (both cherry flavored with cherries in them and regular).

Miscellaneous

Guests can be encouraged to wear red and I chose to hand out gift bags with the usual Valentine's Day giveaways such as love coupons, lotions, body sprays, soaps, aromatic candles and candy.

Memoriam Birthday Roast

One of the greatest coincidences in my life is finding out (years after making these connections) that me, along with my best friends and my boyfriend at the time had birthdays on the same month! We were all going to turn 30 years of age at the same time! We were sick and tired of hearing how we should have already accomplished a long list of things including having a family. In the gay community, anything that is not under thirty, is considered old and many women feel as if the beginning of the rest of their lives start at this same age. WHY?! There is so much pressure to accomplish so many things at a certain time that it makes people feel like complete failures. We all advance in life at our own pace. Just be sure to have aspirations of any kind and take your time accomplishing these.

I was talking to a friend of mine about getting older and about the legacies we could leave behind before we die. Since we were already dead to certain people because we were "so old" and we really enjoyed watching birthday celebrity roasts on TV, I decided we should combine the two.

All of our friends received invitations to a funeral to honor the "memory" of four of my friends and I. They were encouraged to wear black. Only the birthday boys wore all white sporting angel wings to complement the outfit. When guests arrived, they were encouraged to pick a calla lily from the entrance and were served coffee-flavored alcoholic drinks. Calla lilies and coffee are popular choices at funerals. There was a cake in the shape of a crucifix and a real-life coffin right at the center of the stage. The idea behind it was that each birthday boy would have to enter this coffin (open casket) one after the other and endure the criticism of the eulogy (which consisted of drag queens roasting us) as the audience had a laugh at our expense.

Some people feel as if they didn't matter to anyone in the world. This theme party is a great way to make them feel loved and remembered, share a few laughs and raise their self-esteem because it is testament of all the things people always remember when they think of the individuals (guests of horror).

Decorations

The decorations may vary according to the guest. Because of the nature of this theme, the location can be decorated as a church, cemetery, heaven and even hell (if the birthday boy/girl has been bad). I chose Heaven as the theme for this birthday. We all wore angel wings and wore white. The activities center where it was held had white décor everywhere. You may use pillow filling (cotton) to hold small clouds above the tables with fishing wire and insert LED lights inside of them (for lightning effects) or have a holographic projector illustrating images of the skyline on the ceiling. Adding couches, floor-length candelabras, white fabric, smoke machine, harps and white balloons may be added for a more dramatic effect of heaven.

Food

The food served may be anything the birthday boy or girl desires. The cake, in order for it to go along with the theme, can be in the shape of a coffin, cross, headstones or anything that compliments the theme.

Entertainment

This is also up to the guest of honor; however, the roast should be made by friends and relatives of the guest of honor. I had drag queens on my birthday as they always provide a cut-throat and sarcastic way to deliver their lines. It was hilarious! Think of those tombstones at Disney's Haunted Mansion when thinking of funny things to say about the birthday boy/girl. You can also say things like "We know heaven will never be the same now that Kate is there driving every angel crazy with her overactive PMS and constant need to tell everybody what to do!", etc.

Miscellaneous

The guests should be encouraged to wear black (as it is kind of a funeral) and the guest of honor may wear white. I chose to wear angel wings for my birthday. I used a life-size coffin facing upwards, so the audience would get a kick out of me trying to hold my laughs as they roasted me. Many companies who cater to high school proms also provide great décor to be used for the location's entrance.

You may choose to have a host for the evening in case you want to appear lifeless for the duration of the event before the roast. Make sure this person (who will also be your personal assistant) is dressed up as a clergyman or rabbi or any other man of the cloth (according to the guest of honor's religion affiliation)

JERRY PEREZ 1980-2010

If Paris Hilton was Satan incarnated, Jerry would be the little Chihuahua mutt ridding in her purse. Rosario, as he was commonly refer to as (even though he couldn't cook to save his own life), shall always be remembered for his writing abilities, his boring classic movies, and his very active PMS. If we each had a dime for every time Mr. Mood-Swings needed a Midol, we would all be enjoying an early retirement. You can rest assure that someone up there is having a great time listening to Jerry's jokes and ability to rip people to shreds with sarcasm and an apple martini in his hand. Although he has always been the reason why most people take medication and most vehicles are equipped with ejector seats, he was the type of friend you could rely on to act as a psychologist, party planner or task manager. Jerry, we will miss you more than you have missed your long lost fast metabolism. Have fun up there in Cellulite City, you controlling bastard!

LIve

Social Media

Reasons Why Nobody Ever Goes Shopping with Me

Spread'em! See More

Where's Jerry?

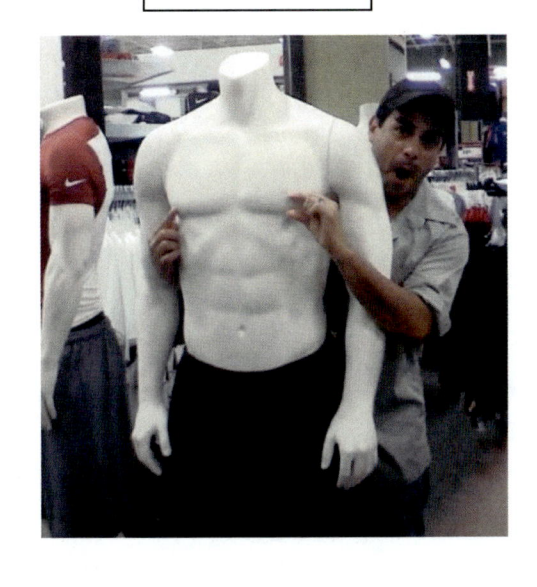

107

Reasons Why I'm Not Invited to Things

This is my step ladder. I never knew my real ladder 😢 — 😊 Feeling silly. See More

I was invited to a pool party. I showed up looking like this. I stood by the pool while swimmers stared at me trying to figure out who I was. I said nothing. I just stood there looking at them and sharpening my eating utensils. I was asked if I wanted a bite to eat. I said: "Thank you, but I had a surfer on the way here. Who knows? I might get hungry later".

I always try to take a souvenir when I stay in hotels.

Blah Blah Bla...

Someone asked me if I was seeing anyone. This is my way to tell them how sexless and uninterested my life is:

> Bruh, in my life, the plumber comes to my house to ACTUALLY fix the plumbing and the pizza delivery guy brings me my pizza with extra sausage and I ACTUALLY tip him with money and he was just there to deliver that box of pizza!

> Ok, Looks like we still have some work to do

> GIVE ME BACK MY WAFFLE

> BTW, Harlot is Harley's thing. My dog is Harley, the harlot

> We're all harlots, btw.

> You get nothing and like it

> WAFFLE

> No!

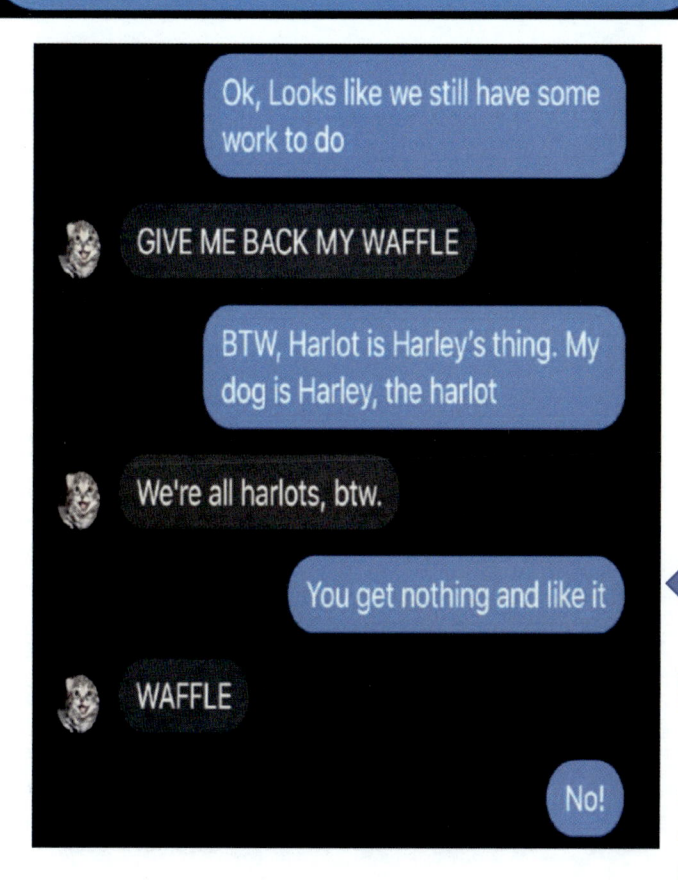

My friend and I were talking about the "new addition" to the family. I asked if he wanted to meet my daughter and then sent a photo of my dog, Harley.

> dog!

> Yes! Very good! Good boy! And what is this called?

> HARLOT
> WITCH

Jerry Perez
Jan 26, 2013 · Fort Lauderdale, FL

The Walking Dead has taught me that a true friend is he who will shoot you in the face when the right time comes. To all those who I consider my true friends... I love you very much so, make sure you get it right on the first shot or I will eat you. Nom nom nom... Friends are great (with a little salt)

> My friend and I were talking about the type of guys she likes to date. She's attracted to what is referred to as the "thug look"

Jerry Perez
How come every guy that you are attracted to makes me feel I should be locking my car doors when I drive by them at the red light or get a tighter grip on my purse when they sit next to me in church? 🤔 lol
1h   Like   Reply

Jerry Perez um he has a intimidating look on him. However you would love his band it's all rock music the band is called Bad Apple
3m   Like   Reply

Jerry Perez
Now I know for sure I am getting older. I just had this thought: "what's this?! ████ What's the name of your hot song? F███ You, Recycling or That's Not my Bag of Coke, Officer!" 😂

> My friend was commenting on a present I mailed to him and said "You're awesome!" This was my response...

Jerry Perez
██████ I know, right?! That's what I keep saying...

...to myself...

...in front of a mirror...

I believe that if I keep repeating things in front of a mirror, they come true.
2m   Like   Reply

Write a reply...

Jerry Perez
Wait a second...
2m   Like   Reply

Jerry Perez
That means...
2m   Like   Reply

Jerry Perez
Beetlejuice, Beetlejuice, Beetlejuice!!!

The officer said, "You drinking?"
I said, "You buying?"
We just laughed and laughed. I need bail money.

ROTTENeCARDS

Omg! This just blew my mind. I was watching this movie and noticed "hey! Johnny Depp's bodyguard in the movie can slap me around and call me a bitch any time he wants! Could this be...love?"

So, I have to know...why the request? Did I seem that interesting? Lol

8:22 AM

We had some mutual friends and you popped up as a suggested friend.

10:17 AM

That's my thing. I'm always popping out of everything: Facebook friend requests, garbage cans, my mom...

Not sure how they pulled that off...

(Holy Bible — SIGNED COPY)

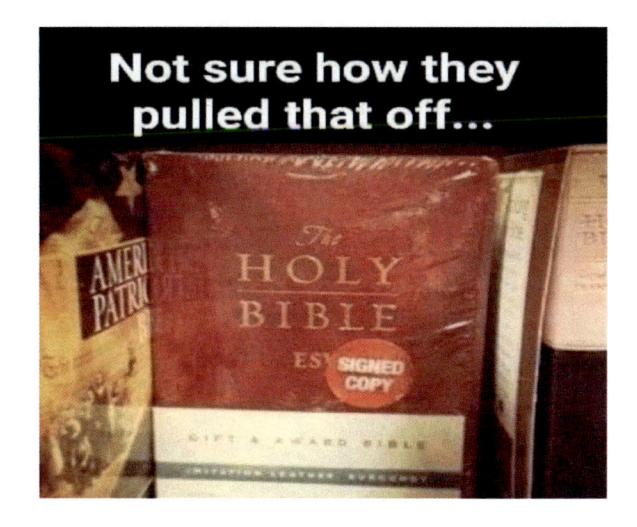

Green Pork Meat??!! So....basically, if you eat me, you will die 😂

Your Stripper name is the color of your underwear and the last thing you ate.

Jerry Perez
Mar 18, 2012 · Wilton Manors, FL

I wore green down to my underwear and kissed 7 Irish guys...please tell me that's good luck! Otherwise I will loose faith on the whole "kiss me, I'm Irish" thing!

BEWARE OF THE DANCING RESTROOM FREAK!!!

This is the 10th time I've been warned about a mysterious dancing man who apparently lurks in every public restroom. I'm thinking maybe he dry-humps you while you're standing at the urinal or dances behind you while you look in the mirror. Whenever I see this crazy dancing man sign, I stop and then slowly walk away to the next available bathroom. Beware friends! You could be his next victim! (Eerie music)

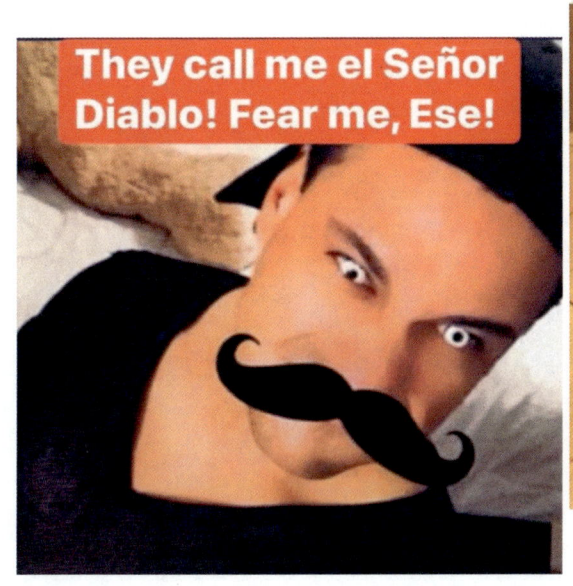

They call me el Señor Diablo! Fear me, Ese!

(CAUTION / CUIDADO / ATTENTION)

111

"Pen is broken. Please use finger"

THE PAIN OF BEING A BOOK-ADDICT

PAPERBACKS — GETS TOO EASILY DAMAGED

HARDCOVERS — TOO HEAVY TO READ IN BED

KINDLE — DOESN'T HAVE SMELL OF BOOKS

I was asked to set these tables at a restaurant I was working at. Obviously, my mind was somewhere

I'm baking brownies with my friend last night and he tells me: "Jerry, why is it that everything translated to Spanish is so dirty?! It says here that is 'muy caliente to work on the vulva and makes you horny'. You guys are always so insatiable!" As I read the instructions, I teach him the correct pronunciation of 'caliente', 'revuelva' and 'hornee' 😂 I tell him "when was the last time you saw me getting 'caliente' over any 'vulva'?! Seriously!" LOL

112

I just thought of a word and I need your help trying to get it to catch on! There have been some people that I have talked to and some of their posts on social media are hilarious to me. I get that we all work out and feel proud of our achievements, but why not just say that instead of showing photographs of yourself half naked to say something so random at times.?!

Do we need to see all of you? If I'm happy the way my legs turned out, so I'll share a picture of my legs before and after or my chest or my arms hoping I can encourage others to be more physically active. But these people are just peacocks. That's my word! Social media peacocks!

They're not commenting on what they say they want to comment on. They're basically saying "look at me! I'm cute right?!" 😂 I'm not using names or photos of the people I've encountered, so I used some models posing the way they did saying the things the have said. Believe me, I have nothing to be jealous or envious about. It's just funny to watch.

These peacocks are starved for attention and the comments below their photos from others are hilarious because they don't really answer the question they ask or comment on what they are talking about. They just talk about how hot they look 😂

THESE ARE SOCIAL MEDIA PEACOCKS. SPREAD THE WORD!

113

WAIT A MINUTE I NEED TO POST THIS

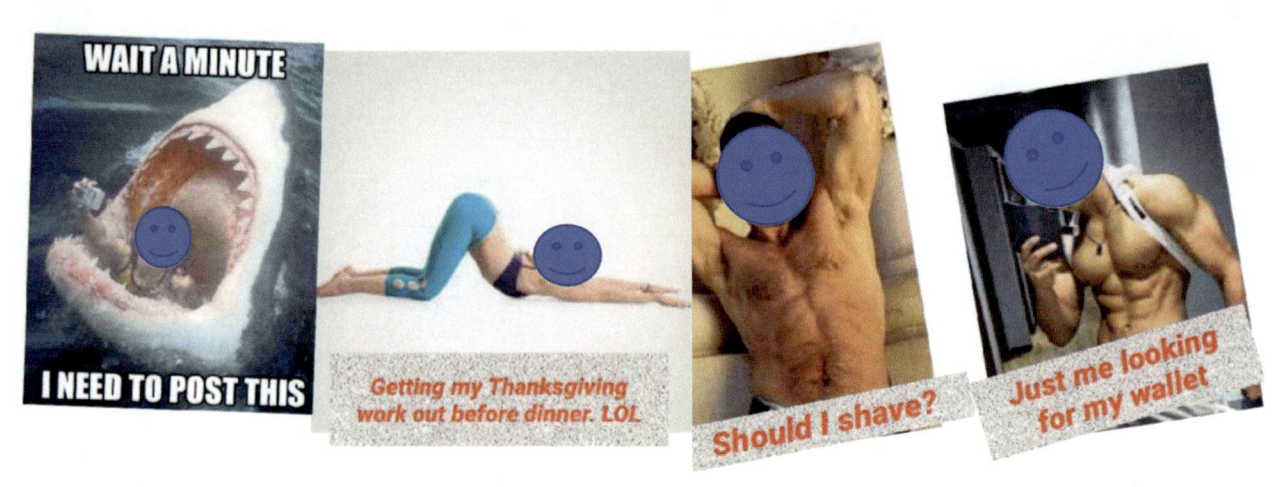

Getting my Thanksgiving work out before dinner. LOL

Should I shave?

Just me looking for my wallet

Enjoying my vacation

Today was brutal. Can't wait to go to bed and have a well-deserved rest.

Ugh! So much work to do today!

Having my coffee. Good morning!

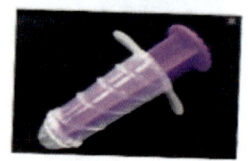

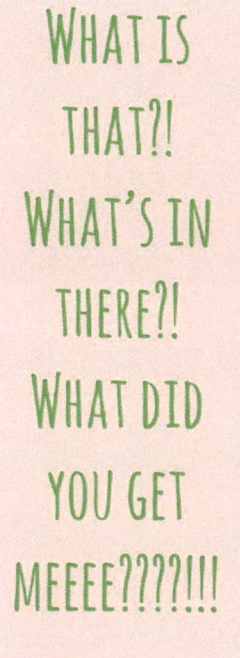

WHAT IS THAT?! WHAT'S IN THERE?! WHAT DID YOU GET MEEEE????!!!

UNICORNS!!! BUT LOOK, I ALSO MADE YOU A... UNICORNS!!!

THANK YOU, DADDY! YOU'RE THE BEST!

I LOVE YOU, SWEETHEART. YOU WANT TO HEAR SOMETHING FUNNY?

NO! UNICORNS! YAY!

My puppy, Harley and her love for unicorns

THERE GRANDMA, I FIXED IT

I am here for you

Thanks :) I'm going through a tough time so it means a lot

And sorry, I lost all my contacts who is this?

This is your Uber driver

I am here to pick you up

Oh

HAVE YOU SEEN THIS MAN?

The NeverEnding Story as a child.

The NeverEnding Story as an adult.

You know "cheese" having an orgasm

Get it? Uh? (elbow nudge)

116

Remember that scene from Bad Moms where they talk about their kids at a restaurant? One of them talks about how her daughter killed her hamster, but they made it look like an accident. "My daughter's a killer" – she says. Well, Harley killed a rat last night. She has killed snakes, frogs, lizards, iguanas, flies, and rodents since I got her. My little girl's a murderer! 😫

Dear lord! Well I think it's safe to say we got a generation of hooker-looking ladies in our future. Thanks a lot, Mattel!

Yes, we are facing a pandemic.
Yes, we are at war due to our political opinions.
Yes, the Kardashians are still relevant.

But how can you be annoyed with anything when looking at a face like this?! I mean, come on! 🐶💓

Good night, everybody!

Well, it finally happened. What every father fears to hear about his daughter. I have spent years teaching this girl how to sit like a lady and now her bad manners are giving her a bad reputation. Now, if you'll excuse me, I gotta go to church and say a hundred Hail Mary's 🙏

My elf is on a wrecking ball! 🎶

And every Christmas tree he'll knock! 🎵

All he wanted was to mess you up! 🎶

Because now he works for Gree-e-en Peace! 🎵

I don't have a fav Christmas movie so tell me yours.

Jerry Perez
Happy Endings and Happy Ho-lidays (wait, I think that was actually an adult film). Oh! How about Going Down in the Chimney? (wait, wait....I think that was a dirty movie too. And I mean DIRTY! Those actors were covered in SO much ash! Why can't I think of a movie? Maybe I'm just a sick pervert. Wait! I got it! A Christmas Story, A Bad Moms Christmas and Christmas with the Kranks. Yay! I'm saved! I'm actually a decent human being!

The dude I met last night at the bar told me he likes it "doggy style" so I brought him home and humped his leg for one hour.

Sweet melons, Batman! Don't you hate it when you're about to hug someone really sexy and then hit yourself in the mirror?! 😂 Seriously though, I'm proud of what I've accomplished so far. I don't have a gym here so it's all natural like Push-ups and sit ups on the grass at the park, swinging from tree branches like some sort of monkey and sprinting like a crazy cat running away from the vacuum cleaner. The best part is... Mi tits are back! Save me a seat, Victoria. I'm coming to buy a couple of secrets from you! Can't wait to use words like "hey! Sir, my eyes are up here" as I point to my face or lean over that counter at the auto repair shop wearing my corset having "my girls" do a pickaboo through my cleavage! I'm gonna be pimping out my titties everywhere I go to get some discounts! Now I'll have to go to the bathroom in pairs with the other pretty girls because that's what we do to avoid sexual assaults. You know, power in numbers. Maybe I'll have them reduced before breastfeeding. I heard that could be a problem. OK, I'm just rambling on this point. Anyway! Good night Facebook! Good night, friends! Good night, boobs! Take care of yourselves and each other!!!

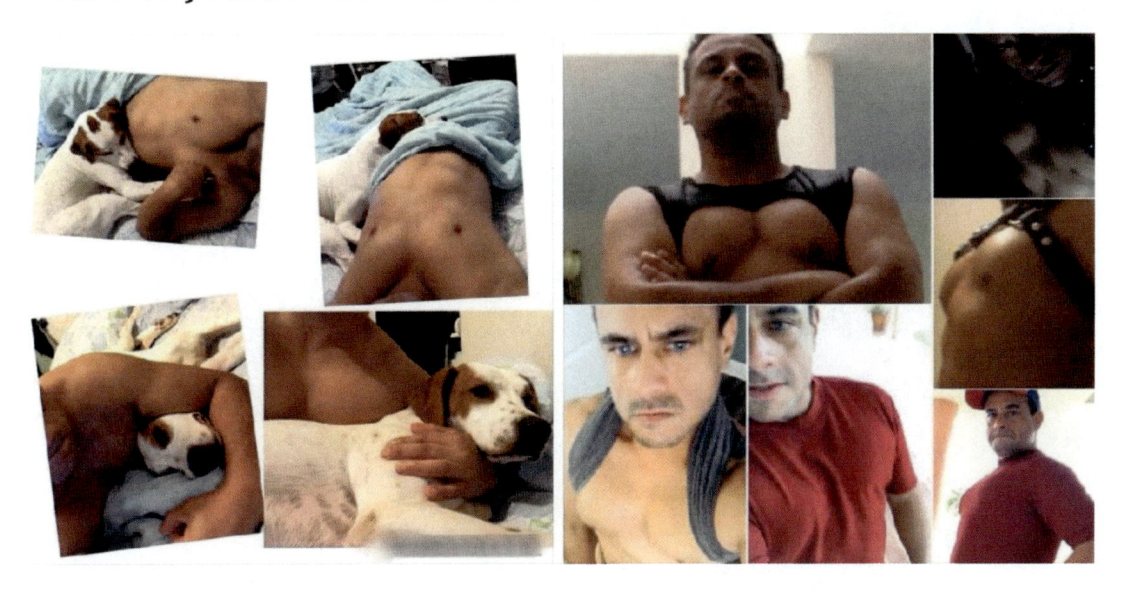

If these dogs were human, this is how I picture them. This is why I named mine Harley. She's like: "Ohhh! A picture! Yeah! Take it! Take it! TAKE IT!!!" Mogwai is more like: "Seriously, dude? Get the hell away from me!"

My dog

MOM'S DOG

Ok, tell me what you think: mom has been using these Santa's heads for years. I think they're the creepiest shit ever! I just hung 25 decapitated heads that belonged to a saint! It's a Christmas tree of death! I showed my aunt and she suggested a hint of red to make it more festive, so I grabbed a bottle of ketchup and walked towards the severed heads and...well, you do the math. The bloody effect didn't sit well with mom, so I left it as they were. Hey! I can actually utter the phrase "I got a little head" and not imply anything fun/dirty!

Awww yeah, bitches! We got chocolate chip cookies for all the sluts of the world! 😂 Bimbo cookies, which you can find on the same aisle they carry Trampy Twizzlers and Skanky Cakes 🧁 🍰 🍭 🍪

There is something I need to say. It's been on my mind for a while and I kept questioning if I should talk about this or not. It's of extreme importance and it has been responsible for many battles between people in the past. No one ever has the courage to speak up, but I will be brave enough to point it out because it needs to be said and I don't care who I offend with this. I really don't and I know it sounds cruel, but it has been bothering me for years!

It's about time we talk about this so, I will just go ahead and speak my mind! I hate to be controversial, but...

THE TOILET PAPER FLAP (the first ply) NEEDS TO FACE FORWARD, NOT BACKWARDS!

Yeah! That's right! I said it!

I got mad babysitting skills. Why do people always complain that it's hard?! I had no issues with the niece. All you need is a bowl of water and you're good to go. Interested? Call me at 1-800-BIG-CAGE.

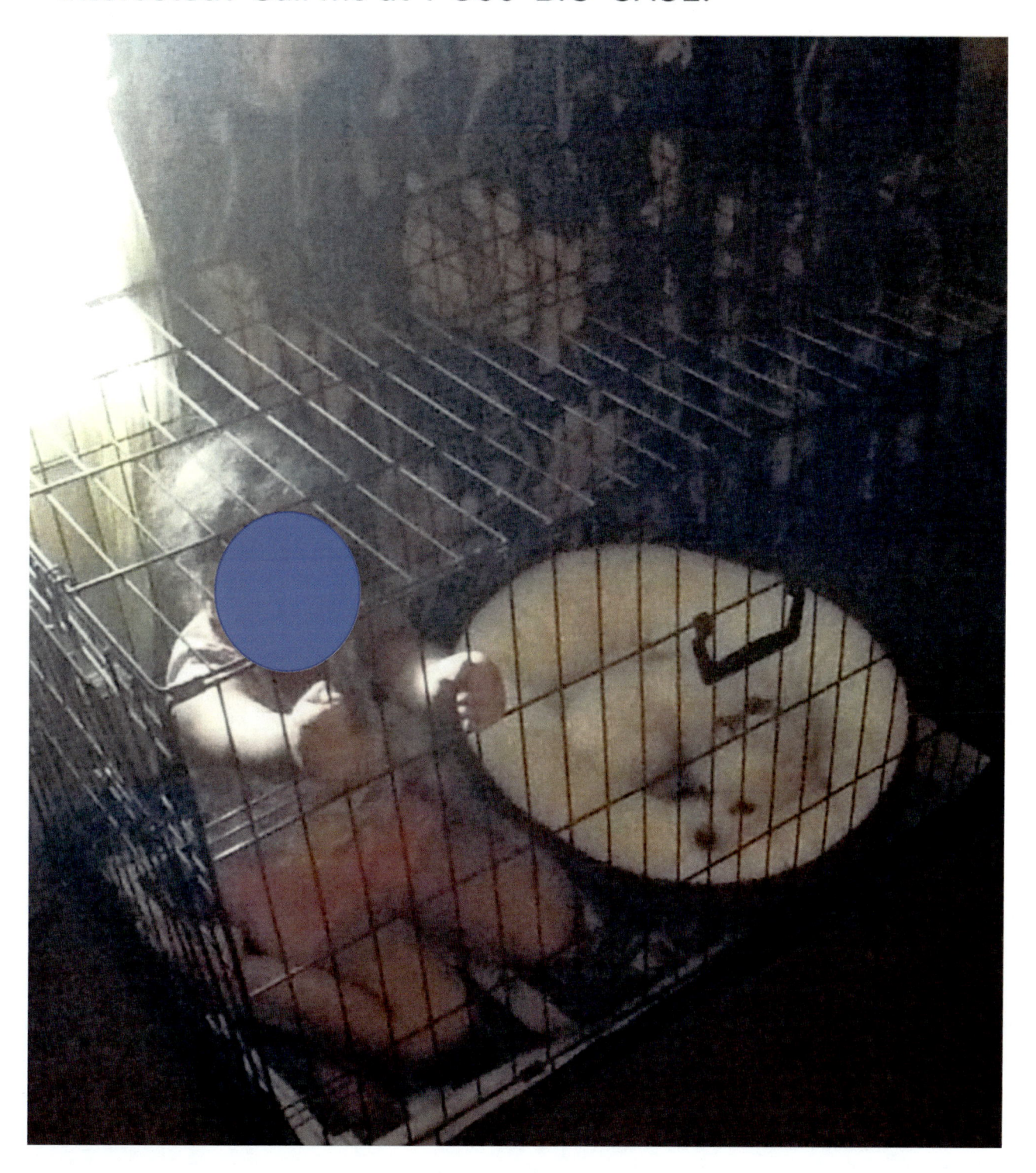

Mom had this fake tree in her house and she always said she wanted to throw it away. I covered its imaginary ears and told mom to not say it too loud because it could hurt its feelings because, well...I'm an idiot. I had a heart to heart with the fake tree, gave it a makeover and moved it to a different location.

> My friend asked me why I like Wonder Woman so much

Jerry Perez
[name] it's not your fault. I'm not sure if you're aware of this, but Wonder Woman is the queen of Gay Geekdom.
1m Like Reply

Jerry Perez
[name] we were all twirling around and pretending we have superpowers since we were 5! Lol
Just now Like Reply

Jerry Perez
That is a perfect imitation of what I did as a kid. Only thing missing is me doing this in a tank top and bikini underwear with a long extension cord attached to the side of my waist. 😂
Just now Like Reply

If your cell phone is smart do this but change the pilot.

[helicopter emoji art]

😀😂 2   15 Comments

Like   Comment   Share

[reply] ...See More

View 1 previous reply...

View 1 more reply...

Jerry Perez
☐ ■ ☑ ⭕
NAILED IT!

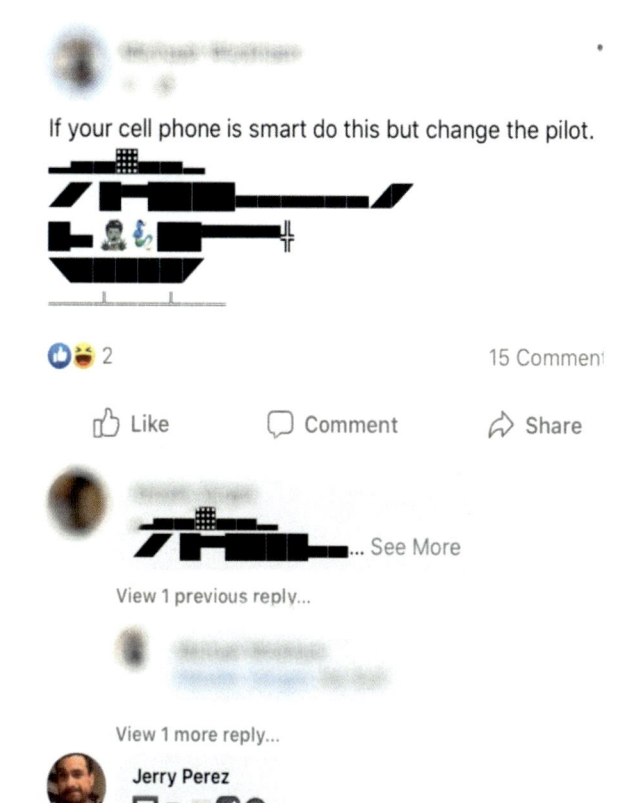

Three phrases I have learned to hate: "excuse me" at the bus stop at night, "trust me" in LA, "this won't hurt a bit" at the dentist's office

127

Every time I go through a break up, I look forward to my "Sandra Dee" moment from the movie Grease. You know... Showing up at the fair with a make over wearing black leather and looking all hot and sexy while every one desires you... Damn I'm gay!

Finally got my awesome gay uncle uniform shirt. We're like their dads...only cooler 😜 My niece obviously approves #GunclesRock

This tree screams masculinity! Yes, there are a few unicorn figurines in there. It's butch A. F. ,bro! It's like I'll see it walking by at Home Depot beating the crap out of professional wrestlers who happened to be there shopping on the same day this tree decided to wreck havoc on us with its macho massacre!

Then, I can totally see this tree playing poker and figuring out a way to add Russian Roulette to the mix and win! This tree would make Chuck Norris piss his pants! I pity the fool who crosses paths with this colorful, mean killing machine that reeks of bourbon, Old Spice and sweaty car mechanic's shirt after doing an oil change under the hot sun in Calcutta! Grrrrrr!

Hail Satan! 😈 When you push down the pump, it comes out red, so you sanitize your hands with the blood of the innocent, then you hear heavy metal playing in the background (but backwards) and Ozzy Osbourne comes out of a corner and bites the head off a bat. But hey...at least we're staying safe. Oh! Also, Freddy Krueger massacres you if you're not wearing your protective mask 🤘 HELL YEAH, BITCHES!!!!

Harley is crazy about wearing scarves. She loves them! She think she's the most beautiful thing on the planet and gets so mad when I take them off, so I decided to make her two of these. I'm going to hand-stitch them and glue things to it. Shhhh... You can't say anything! Keep it a secret from her!

Feel like having a laugh at my expense? Bro! My back and shoulders are killing me today! Don't feel bad for me. It's my fault. I get this "superhero feeling" every time someone seems to be in need of something...let's say for example: a lady carrying a heavy duffel bag at the hotel I work for. It goes something like this:

Me - Good evening, Miss! Can I help you with those? Stupid weak lady who shouldn't be carrying so much crap for one stupid weekend - Oh, thank you! They are heavy though.
Me - It's ok, I'm sure I can handle one bag! Please, have a sit and relax.

As I began to carry it, I noticed she was definitely a serial killer who just finished stuffing her last 10 victims inside that bag so I carried it still with a fake smile on my face as a poor substitute for an attempt to hide the tears of suffering denying my torment and the hernia from hell felt at the time because, you know....I'M A MAN, DAMN IT!!! Grrrrr!) 😂

I am now at the dealership for my routine car maintenance sitting on a special chair (I'm guessing it's there for the elderly or idiots like me) as I write this. It's gonna be 2 freaking hours! Thank god they sell the food of my people here! Lol. It's like god just walked over to me wearing his "chanclas" and handed me these deep-fried pieces of sin as he whispered in y ear that everything will be alright...yeah...these empanadas are THAT GOOD! 😂

Batman in Puerto Rico

There was a battle in Puerto Rico between doctors and the citizens of this country. Every store you walked into was required to take your temperature because of the COVID-19 virus. However, they were taking the temperature in the wrong area of the body: the shoulders, forearms and back of your hand simply because there was a rumor stating that the infrared laser from the detector affected your cornea and brainwaves. It was ridiculous! When mom and I entered one of these supermarkets where you buy things in bulk, we suggested they "shoot" the laser on our forehead. Usually, they agree to this request, but these people, not only refused, but took my mother's arm by force to be scanned. She replied: "Listen, I have been a doctor for over 30 years, and I want to instruct you on this because you may be letting people in who might be feverish and not know because your arm temperature is a lot cooler". The girl at the entrance simply said: "Move along". I was furious. I refused to have my arm taken and she told the bouncer not to allow me inside. I said to him: "Go ahead, I dare you put your hands on me like you guys did to my mother!" They kept fighting me, so I reminded them that what they were doing was an assault and I would inform the authorities, which I did. No one cared around there. I was so scared! This guy was huge and I'm just a little angry Chiwawa dog compared to him. The girl said to me: "Just go ahead". I replied: "That's what I thought! Let's go mom" – "Get away from me, I don't know you!" was what she said to me. She was embarrassed but standing up to those morons made my day. This means war! The next day I dressed up as Batman (on vacation) and made a flyer indicating how to do these things correctly. I wrote THE JOKERS OF THE WORLD DO THINGS INCORRECTLY. BE A HERO. I dressed up my mom's dog as Robin (to be more approachable and earn the public's affection) and, hopefully, saved a few lives in the process.

NO PERMITAS QUE TE TOMEN LA TEMPERATURA EN EL BRAZO!

Desde que somos niños y sentimos fiebre, el tacto va DIRECTAMENTE a tu frente o a tus mejillas para verificar si en verdad se siente que tienes fiebre. USA EL SENTIDO COMÚN!

Consulta con cualquier **oculista** si el artefacto para tomar la temperatura hace daño a la retina de los ojos por el láser infrarojo y te dirán que esto NO ES CIERTO! No temas rumores falsos! Puerto Rico es uno de 4 lugares EN EL MUNDO que hace esto.

Sé el héroe en contra de este virus. **Los GUASONES del mundo hacen las cosas incorrectamente.**

Para más información sobre esto, hable con su médico y dele las gracias por todo lo que hacen por nosotros! Los médicos son nuestros héroes en esta batalla y tienen el conocimiento necesario para combatir esto. El aceptar métodos erróneos en las tiendas, te expone a estar en contacto con personas que pueden estar infectadas y no tener conocimiento de esto. La temperatura de tu brazo siempre va a ser más baja que la de la frente porque la lectura es INCORRECTA. Protégete a ti y a los tuyos y unámonos en contra de la ignorancia y la pandemia! No empeores las cosas ahora que estamos tan cerca de terminar esta pesadilla! (Dile a todos! Corre la voz!)

Batman

134

Text 1 (spam exchange):

> Do you want to know how amaze girls in the bedroom? This will make IT Rock Hard for 4 hours at least. Grow 3 inches in a week!

> Mine's the size of an outie bellybutton. Your product will only give me 4 inches in a week! Oh wow! I can't wait to go out rocking my mini tanned one-eyed bald menace and make the bastard puke baby juice all over some hot models!

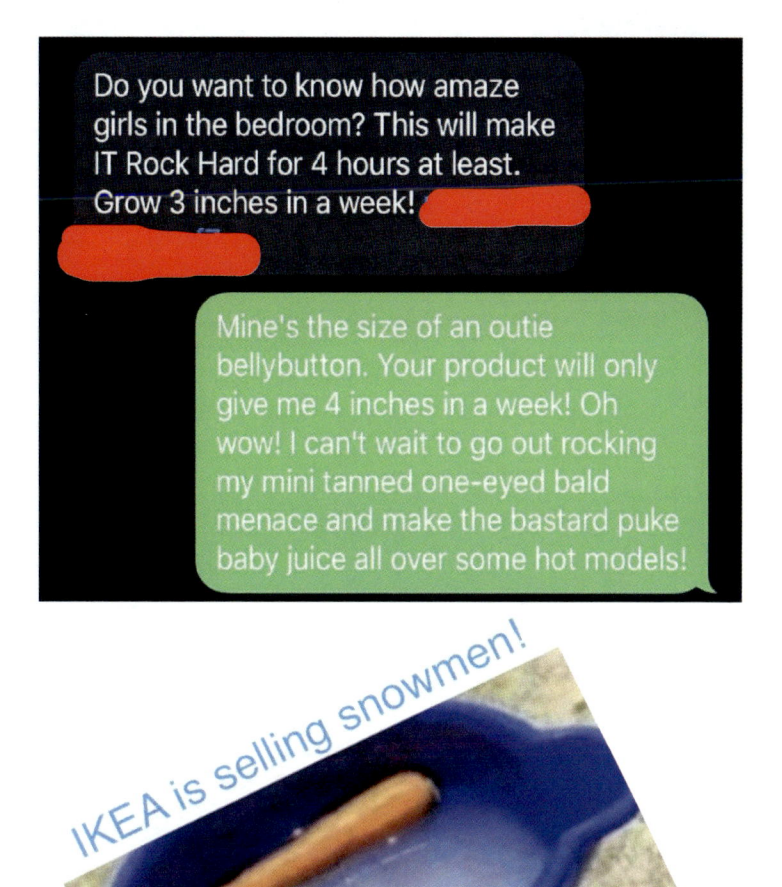

How to frighten the new generation:

Put them in a room with a rotary phone, an analog watch, and a TV with no remote. Then leave directions on how to use in cursive.

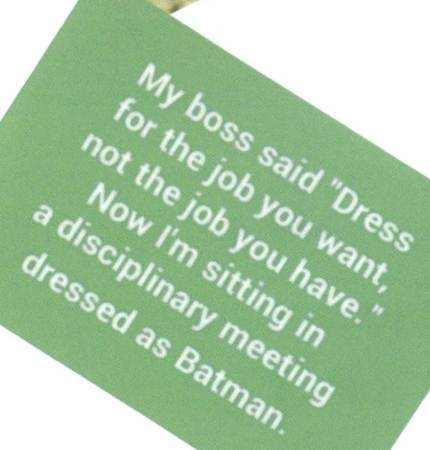

IKEA is selling snowmen!

My boss said "Dress for the job you want, not the job you have." Now I'm sitting in a disciplinary meeting dressed as Batman.

BUT DAD, ALL THE OTHER KIDS LEAVE COOKIES AND MILK FOR HIM.

TRUST ME ON THIS SON, I KNOW WHAT SANTA WANTS.

Well, hello there Nightmares! I was wondering what you were up to!

Steampunk Tendencies
Dec 16, 2019
Cat photo taken in the 1800's

You know you're in love when you look at everything you posses and realize nothing belongs to you anymore... Not even your heart. (except for my action figures collection! I'll cut the bitch who touches those! LOL)

It all makes sense now. Gay marriage and marijuana are being legalized at the same time.
Leviticus 20:13 says if a man lays with another man, he should be stoned.
We were just misinterpreting it.

Dear lord! 8 glasses of water a day feels like having Lake Michigan in your stomach!

When u supposed to be on ur New Years diet and ur dog starts judging you

Wishing you all a great VD! (hope it's syphilis or something very itchy) he he he ;-)

I've decided I'm bisexual. I love my baby, but now I'm starting to love my SIRI a lot more!!!

★

Less tongue, please! I'm a vegetarian

★

That's just too obvious. Evil is not even trying anymore. Lol

THIS CHOCOLATE DORA CLEARLY WANTS MY SOUL

Being kissed while you are asleep is one of the purest forms of love... Unless you are in prison.

Whatever you give a woman, she will make greater. Give her sperm she will make a baby, give her a house she will give you a home, give her groceries she will give you a meal, give her a smile she will give you her heart. She multiplies and enlarges what she is given. So if you give her any crap, be ready to receive a ton of shit!

Nothing like a pair of chopsticks to make even Cheetos look fancy. Move away Martha Stewart! I got this one

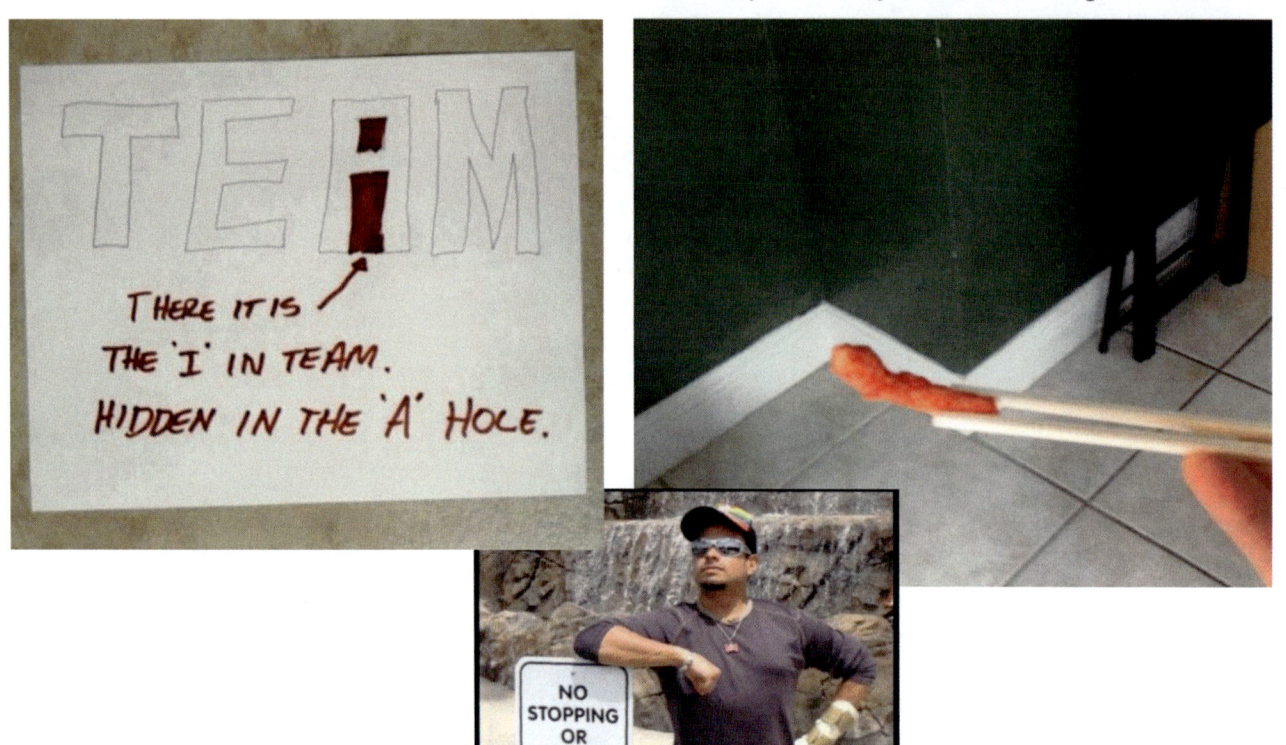

THERE IT IS
THE 'I' IN TEAM.
HIDDEN IN THE 'A' HOLE.

I've never felt more rebellious!

I'm a vegetarian now. Well, actually I'll eat fish so I think the term is pecatarian...? Yes, I'll get my protein from sea food (plus the occasional chicken every now and then...and beef). You know what? Now that I think about it, I don't think I'm a vegetarian at all. Forget I said anything.

Dog's Diary

8:00 am – Dog food! My favorite thing!
9:30 am – A car ride! My favorite thing!
9:40 am – A walk in the park! My favorite thing!
10:30 am – Got rubbed and petted! My favorite thing!
12:00 pm – Milk bones! My favorite thing!
1:00 pm – Played in the yard! My favorite thing!
3:00 pm – Wagged my tail! My favorite thing!
5:00 pm – Dinner! My favorite thing!
7:00 pm – Got to play ball! My favorite thing!
8:00 pm – Wow! Watched TV with the people! My favorite thing!
11:00 pm – Sleeping on the bed! My favorite thing!

Cat's Diary

Day 983 of My Captivity

My captors continue to taunt me with bizarre little dangling objects. They dine lavishly on fresh meat, while the other inmates and I are fed hash or some sort of dry nuggets. Although I make my contempt for the rations perfectly clear, I nevertheless must eat something in order to keep up my strength.

The only thing that keeps me going is my dream of escape. In an attempt to disgust them, I once again vomit on the carpet. Today I decapitated a mouse and dropped its headless body at their feet. I had hoped this would strike fear into their hearts, since this clearly demonstrates my capabilities. However, they merely made condescending comments about what a "good little hunter" I am. Bastards!

There was some sort of assembly of their accomplices tonight. I was placed in solitary confinement for the duration of the event. However, I could hear the noises and smell the food. I overheard that my confinement was due to the power of "allergies." I must learn what this means, and how to use it to my advantage.

Today I was almost successful in an attempt to assassinate one of my tormentors by weaving around his feet as he was walking. I must try this again tomorrow, but at the top of the stairs.

I am convinced that the other prisoners here are flunkies and snitches. The dog receives special privileges. He is regularly released, and seems to be more than willing to return. He is obviously retarded. The bird must be an informant. I observe him communicating with the guards regularly. I am certain that he reports my every move. My captors have arranged protective custody for him in an elevated cell, so he is safe . . . for now.

Found a new hiding place for my pup's new chew toy

How Twilight was written.

To be read in Spanish

139

140

LOST UNICORN:

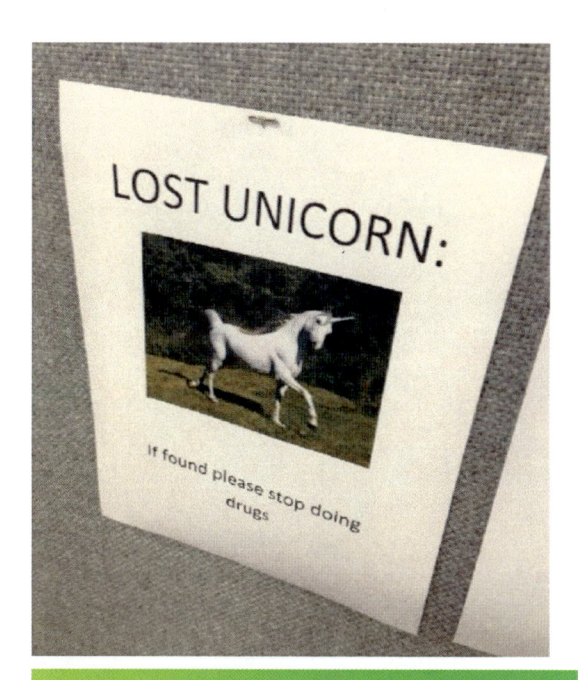

If found please stop doing drugs

Banker Cat does not approve ur loan.

How do you feel wen sumwun coreks youre grammer or speling erurs on Facebooc?

I'm grinding my teeth as I post this! 😬 lol

SEDUCTIVE CAT IS SEDUCTIVE

most cats look down at you, questioning your intelligence

not this one

WHEN THE CAT IS PLOTTING TO KILL YOU AND THE DOG IS TRYING TO WARN YOU...

WAIT A MINUTE... THIS ISN'T THE PARK.

TENTICKLES

According to this book

I can't read!

LOSING YOUR TEETH IN..

3... 2... 1...

WE'RE ALL GONNA DIE.

RIGHT HERE

FIRE IS HOT

I also got a new *meaningful and deep* tattoo
If you care to ask, you may choose the "Water is Wet" or "Rocks are Har... See More

---

I'm watching a movie

What movie?

It's about a mans wife who is brutally murdered by a serial killer and his son is left physically disabled. In a twisted turn of events his son is kidnapped and the dad has to track and chase the kidnapper thousands of miles with the help of a mentally disabled woman.

Oh wow

It's finding nemo

I COULDN'T AFFORD TO TAKE THE KIDS TO SEA WORLD

SO I TOOK THEM TO THE FISH MARKET AND SAID "SHHH THEY'RE SLEEPING."

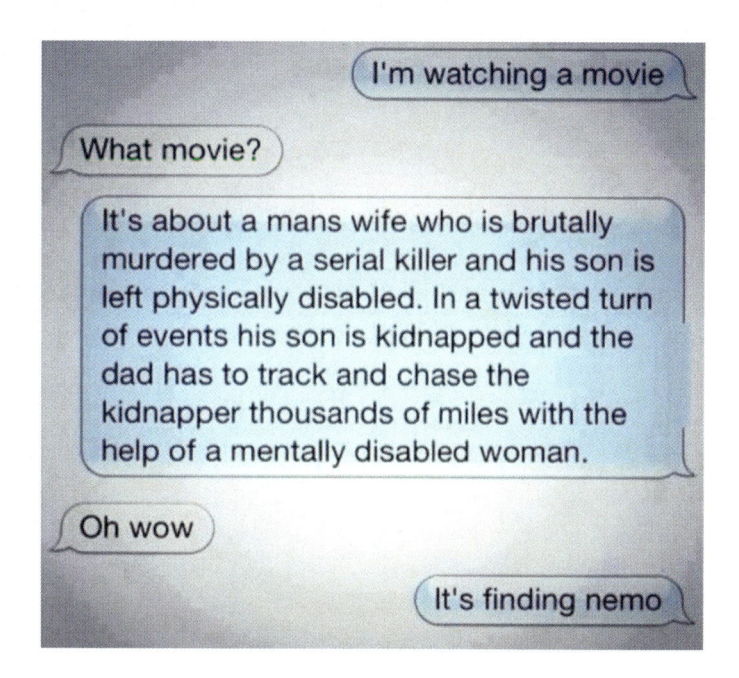

Got up with really messed up hair, so I put the first hat I saw. Unfortunately, it was a hat shaped like a birthday cake that I have used on my birthdays before.

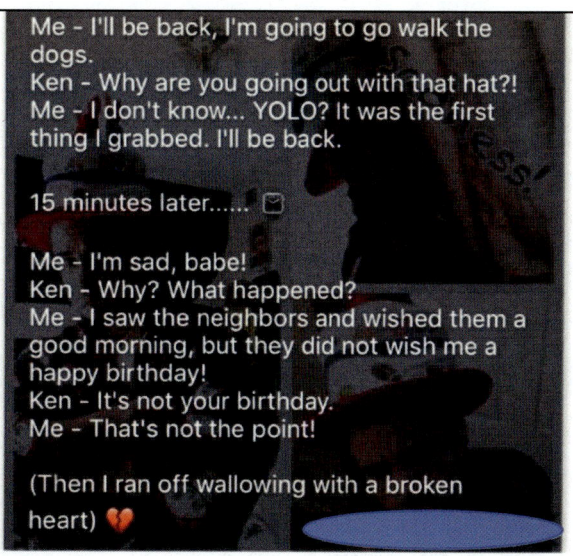

Me - I'll be back, I'm going to go walk the dogs.
Ken - Why are you going out with that hat?!
Me - I don't know... YOLO? It was the first thing I grabbed. I'll be back.

15 minutes later......

Me - I'm sad, babe!
Ken - Why? What happened?
Me - I saw the neighbors and wished them a good morning, but they did not wish me a happy birthday!
Ken - It's not your birthday.
Me - That's not the point!

(Then I ran off wallowing with a broken heart) 💔

143

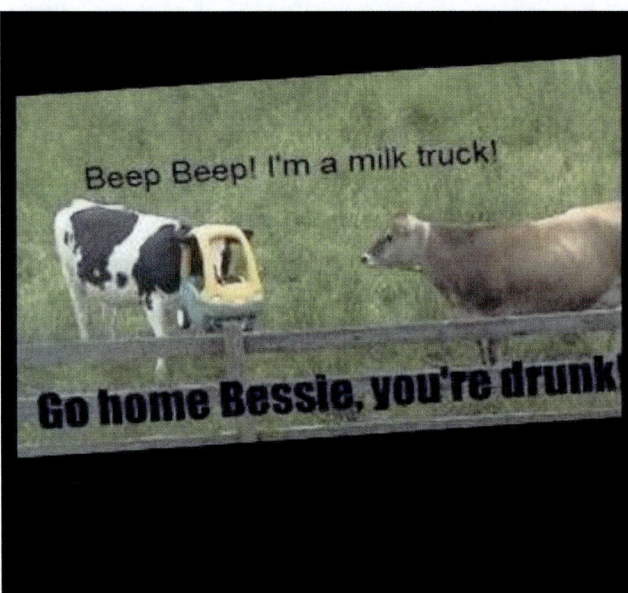

You're Drunk!

Go home, Home!

GOOD EXAMPLE OF A BRAIN STUDY. IF YOU
CAN READ THIS YOU HAVE A STRONG MIND.

7H15 M3554G3
53RV35 7O PR0V3
H0W 0UR M1ND5 C4N
D0 4M4Z1NG 7H1NG5!
1MPR3551V3 7H1NG5!
1N 7H3 B3G1NN1NG
17 WA5 H4RD BU7
N0W, 0N 7H15 LIN3
Y0UR M1ND 1S
R34D1NG 17
4U70M471C4LLY
W17H 0U7 3V3N
7H1NK1NG 4B0U7 17,
B3 PROUD! 0NLY
C3R741N P30PL3 C4N
R3AD 7H15.
PL3453 5H4R3 1F
U C4N R34D 7H15.

SAFE SEX

No toilet paper...goodbye socks!

There is no other logical reasoning behind this other than the fact that I am not a good morning person. The client and banquet manager at the job site today starting at 6am (in Disney!) had a laugh at my expense because of two attempts I made to communicate with this cardboard cutout of a NAVY soldier. Yes...not once, but TWICE!!! The first time was to advise him to take a seat so we could start breakfast and then (forgetting all about my realization earlier) I offered him some coffee. It looks so real though! I should've drank the whole pot of coffee myself before work!

We'll begin with a box, and the plural is boxes,
But the plural of ox becomes oxen, not oxes.
One fowl is a goose, but two are called geese,
Yet the plural of moose should never be meese.
You may find a lone mouse or a nest full of mice,
Yet the plural of house is houses, not hice.

If the plural of man is always called men,
Why shouldn't the plural of pan be called pen?
If I speak of my foot and show you my feet,
And I give you a boot, would a pair be called beet?
If one is a tooth and a whole set are teeth,
Why shouldn't the plural of booth be called beeth?

Then one may be that, and three would be those,
Yet hat in the plural would never be hose,
And the plural of cat is cats, not cose.
We speak of a brother and also of brethren,
But though we say mother, we never say methren.
Then the masculine pronouns are he, his and him,
But imagine the feminine: she, shis and shim!

SIMPLE TRUTH 1
Lovers help each other undress before sex.
However after sex, they always dress on their own.
Simple Truth: In life, no one helps you once you're screwed.

SIMPLE TRUTH 2
When a lady is pregnant, all her friends touch her stomach and say, "Congrats".
But, none of them touch the man's penis and say, "Good job".
Simple Truth: Some members of a team are never appreciated.

FIVE Other Simple Truths
1. Money cannot buy happiness, but it's more comfortable to cry in a Corvette than on a bicycle.
2. Forgive your enemy, but remember the asshole's name.
3. If you help someone when they're in trouble, they will remember you when they're in trouble again.
4. Many people are alive only because it's illegal to kill them.
5. Alcohol does not solve any problems but then neither does milk.

Bonus Truth:
Condoms don't guarantee safe sex. A friend of mine was wearing one when he was shot by the woman's husband.

★

I thought the wedding I just worked was Filipino, but it turned out to be Cambodian. I realized this when I saw Angelina Jolie snatch one of the kids and then darted outside while screaming "Brad, start the car"!!!

> I reacted to a video I was seeing about a celebrity walking us through her walk-in closet. It was huge and operated by a remote control!

Ok, now I am certainly sure that I am gay because I had the following reactions to this video: First, my initial reaction was to strangle her and hate her guts out of jealousy, but why?! I wear MEN's clothes and shoes and I couldn't care less about handbags. Then, I creamed my pants picturing me laying on all those couches and eating shit with my dogs in there as if that were an apartment or something. Lastly, I'd like to say that ACCEPTANCE was my last reaction, but it wasn't. Oh no...not me. Instead I grabbed a bucket of ice cream and sat on the couch as I watched Real Housewives and cried myself into a fattening future over the misery I feel because I don't have a closet like that?! WTF? I have a penis and a 4-bedroom pool home!!! What is happening to me? I feel like I'm the lead in one of those werewolf movies, but instead of body hair and fangs I grow long locks of hair and cherry-red nails and makeup to then rob a music store, grab a microphone and walk around town saying "work it, bitch" as I snap my fingers. I feel a transformation taking over me. I'm fearing the next full moon. **#werequeen** or **#he**-shewolf or **#dragwolf** or **#fullmoonshade**

I love these hashtags. LMAO! 🤩😂

⭐

Rough day today. Started horseback riding and almost fell off it and broke my neck. Then I was allowed to drive a race car and it was so exciting seeing people cheering me on and taking my picture... but suddenly I ran out of quarters so I had to get back to shopping at the mall before the stores closed.

They say you are what you eat. I just can't seem to remember eating a slice of "awesome" last night... 🤔

⭐

I am a full-time gay, but it's so time consuming and expensive. I figured I could downsize to a part-time gay position in which I could still fancy cute guys and clothes, but have enough time and money to do things the sacred scriptures ask of me such as marrying a woman, having kids and living a life of quiet desperation and oppression with the occasional suicidal attempts.

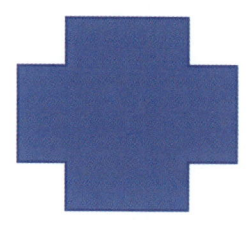

✚

Stressful day at work today! It is now 11pm and I am finally getting the flying (rhymes with duck) outta here!

I would've typed a curse word, but I just joined a convent so I gotta stay pure and shit.

FUCK! I just said "shit"!

SHIT! I just said "fuck"!

So........I've been thinking.... it may be a good time to reconsider this whole "joining a convent-thingy" 🤔

I just realized something...Emma Thompson, Emma Stone and Emma Watson have been in both dramatic and comedic roles. Also Chris Prat, Chris Hemsworth and Chris Evans have been in action/adventure movies and have also played a superhero character.

You know what this means, right? ...

I'M BORED AS F****! 😂

⭐

Doing event for The BoyScouts of America (a.k.a. The keep him busy while mommy has a martini - program). There are so many of them, you'd think it's the Pope's birthday! Yes, I went there. I have a 14-hour shift ahead of me and I'm sick and tired as hell so deal with it! :-)

⭐

It really feels like that old saying about when the universe closes a door, it opens...what was that? A pantry door? Closet? The fly on your pants? Whatever it is, I'm grateful to find good people in the darkest of times. Too many to mention but thank you all for your personal and online support. You make me feel... WINDOW!!! It was a window. Phew! Thank god I got that out of my mind.

Racist jokes time!

Why do Puertorricans don't like blow jobs? - Because they think it may interfere with their unemployment checks

What do you call a Vietnamese family with a living dog? - Vegetarians

Why is Italy shaped like a boot? - Because they couldn't fit all those nymphomaniacs into a sneaker

Be sure not to get the new brand of Jewish tires Firestine. You'll never get anywhere on time as they stop at the sight of a dime and then pick it up.

What is the smallest room in the world? - The Haitian hall of fame

What is the definition of "mixed emotions"? - A Mexican backing off a cliff in your new Mercedes

Too soon...? Ok, here's a lighter non-racist one: An old woman is at the beach with her grandson who is wearing a cute sailor outfit with a matching hat. The waves came in and swept him away when she wasn't looking. Once she noticed what happened she got down on her knees and prayed to god for his return. Instantly, the child returns with another clash of the waves desperately gasping for air. The woman picks him up excitedly and, after careful examination, throws the poor child back in the water yelling: "That isn't him! Mine had a hat!"

God turns water into wine, wine is drank in mass and many celebrations in biblical passages. However, he also created hangovers. Well played, God. He is a wrathful god... A wrathful god indeed...

⭐

Why is it that the AC in my car never works in the summertime? Did I mention my automatic windows stopped being automatic as well? So let me ask you people, how do you like your JERRY cooked? Medium or well done?

⭐

Halloween may be gone, but part of it is still with me... and I don't mean that metaphorically; I am seriously STILL washing green paint out of my ear!!!

⭐

I'm feeling pretty invincible right now. There's no mountain to high to climb and no river too long to travel. Many have been the times I've been beaten by chance but now I have the power to change my own destiny! What I'm trying to say is... I FINALLY advanced to one more level on Candy Crush after being stuck for a whole month!

Why are people so afraid of being honest? Why do people present themselves as something they are not for the sake of making a good first impression? Be yourself from the start and we won't be wasting each other's time. Just let all the crazy out before I commit to having you in my life. With me, what you see is what you get. Ok, so I wear contact lenses sometimes.... and a girdle, but that's it. Nah, I don't wear a girdle, but I do wear a wig...and a prosthetic leg...and a glass eye. I'm just kidding. I don't have any of those things.

But I occasionally put a sock inside my pants.

Got you again!

It's a flashlight :-(

⭐

I think Netflix hates me. Watching this incredibly stupid pile of human excrement titled Sharknado. That's right folks, it's about a tornado filled with sharks. How much pot do you have to smoke to write something like this or even star in it?! Oh wait, Tara Reid is the lead. The world makes sense again.

⭐

This is how I tried to insult a gaymer last night: You are as lame as that first zombie you encounter on every Resident Evil game. You know, the one that's just there as bait to teach you how to use the controller?

New years eve was so amazing I didn't even get a chance to take a photo! Now, here's how I ruined it: someone online reached me (a cute blue eye blonde, as usual). We both agree to be each other's first 2013 kiss so I meet him at the nightclub after work and it was instant attraction. We walked towards each other with a big smile on our faces and, after slowly moving people from our path, we kissed for one minute even before saying "hello". Then we started talking. He said he loved my accent and I tell him I loved his as well. I asked him where he was from because I couldn't recognize the accent's region, to which he replies: "I don't have an accent, I'm deaf"...

Uh...

Earth... When I ask you to swallow me whole, you should just do it! Would've been great last night! Anyways... We are going out on a date ;-P lol

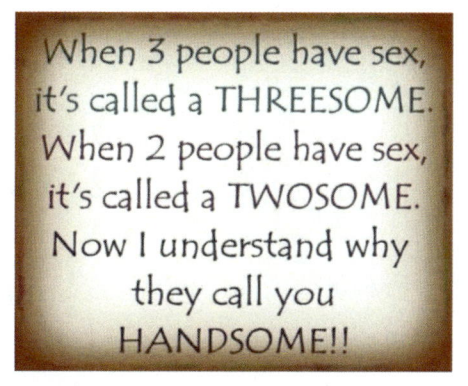

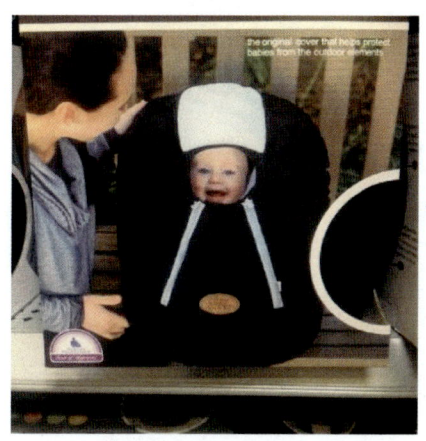

When 3 people have sex, it's called a THREESOME. When 2 people have sex, it's called a TWOSOME. Now I understand why they call you HANDSOME!!

Roses are red,
violets are blue,
sugar is sweet, and so are you.

But the roses are wilting, the violets are dead, the sugar bowl's empty and so is your head.

This is a real product

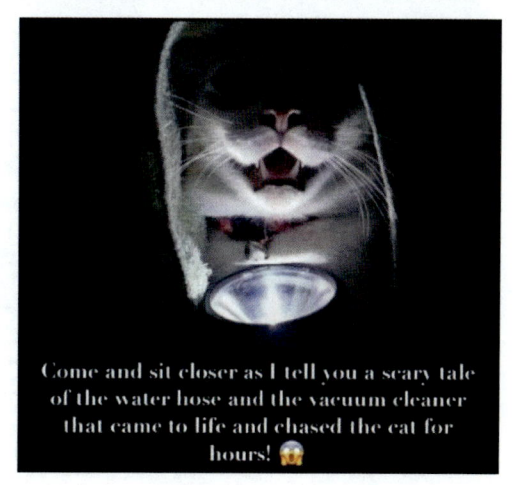

Come and sit closer as I tell you a scary tale of the water hose and the vacuum cleaner that came to life and chased the cat for hours! 😱

This is what happens when you have too much time on your hands. I received a text by mistake from a complete stranger so I thought "what a great way to make new friends!" 😂 I hope I didn't scare her too much.

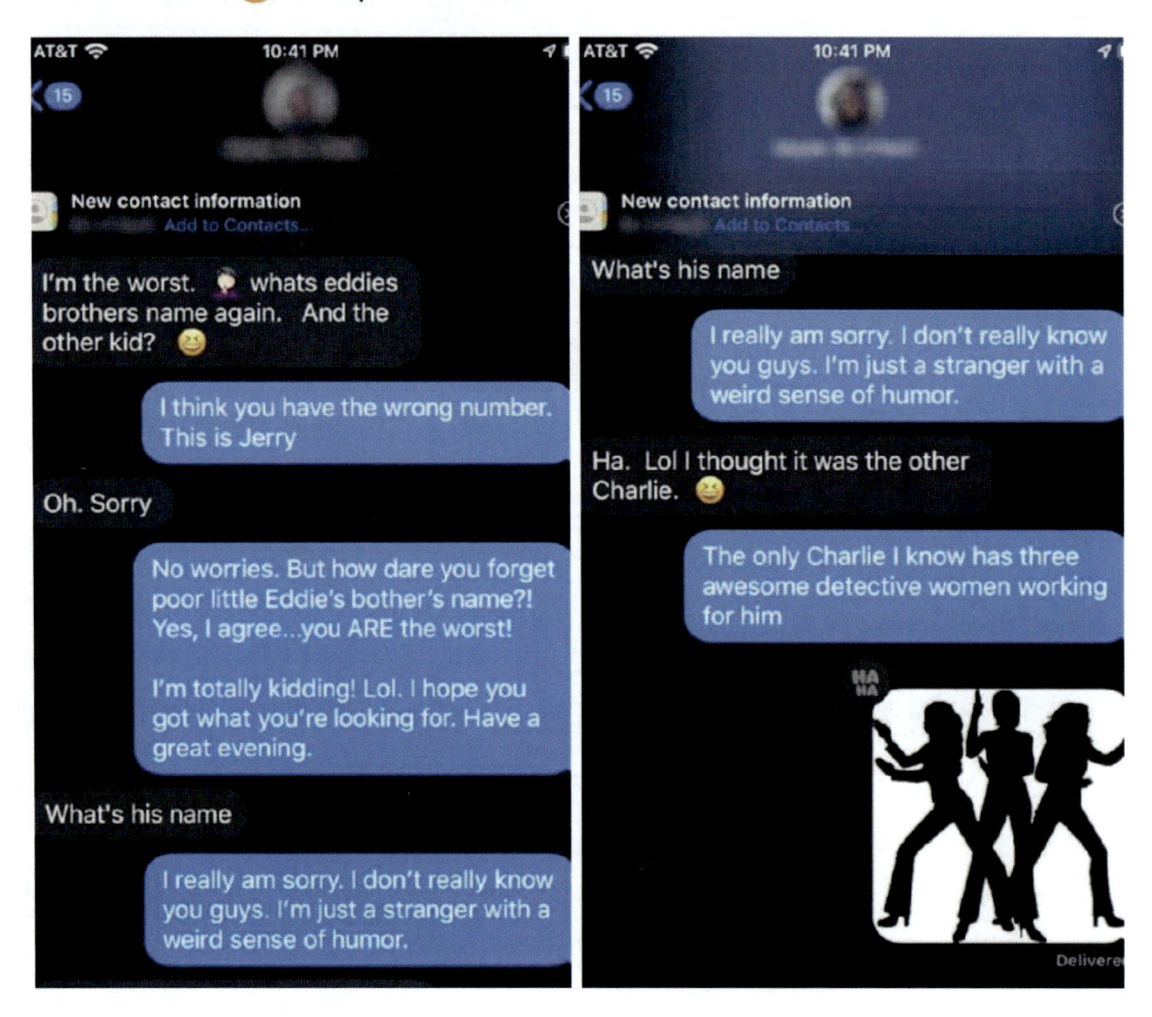

Left conversation:

> I'm the worst. 🙈 whats eddies brothers name again. And the other kid? 😬

>> I think you have the wrong number. This is Jerry

> Oh. Sorry

>> No worries. But how dare you forget poor little Eddie's bother's name?! Yes, I agree...you ARE the worst!

>> I'm totally kidding! Lol. I hope you got what you're looking for. Have a great evening.

> What's his name

>> I really am sorry. I don't really know you guys. I'm just a stranger with a weird sense of humor.

Right conversation:

> What's his name

>> I really am sorry. I don't really know you guys. I'm just a stranger with a weird sense of humor.

> Ha. Lol I thought it was the other Charlie. 😬

>> The only Charlie I know has three awesome detective women working for him

---

So, this only happens every 1,000 years. Take the year you were born and add the age you will be this year! 1984+33=2017!!!!

Did you know that a piranha can devour a small child down to the bone in less than 30 seconds?

Anyways, I lost my job at the aquarium today...

◻

I'm waiting for a voice from above to tell me: "Jerry, you've passed every test. Every tear that you have shed and every aggravation you went through this past year was to prove if you're strong enough and worthy of my rewards. Congratulations, your life from now on, will change for the better. You deserve it". Then again, hearing voices could also mean I'm starting the new year with a severe case of schizophrenia.

◻

Have you ever felt like there is a part of you missing sometimes? Feeling like you were wrong about letting go of something that was special? In your times of weakness, do you not feel you want that back? I know I have and I still do every day... I guess what I am trying to say is... I miss you, carbs! (drops to the floor and cries)

Woke up at 6am for a photo session with Santa for our traditional Holidays Photo Shoots with the family (yes, we are those people) and noticed the initials 'S C' on top of the decor and on every sign leading to the "jolly-candy cane eating-king of commercial Christmas". I was so tired this morning, I asked one of the "elves" there: "Is this decor here to have the children picture themselves in Santa's vacation home in Myrtle Beach?"

She did not understand what could've possessed me to believe such a thing, so I pointed at the signs with the initials S.C. on them as i said "we're in South Carolina, right? Taking a vacation from the North Pole? She said to me: "Those stand for SANTA CLAUS and he would not be on vacation this time of year" 😂 I was so embarrassed! I told her I hadn't had my coffee yet... but the truth is... I don't even drink coffee! So I'm probably just an idiot 😭 (runs away in tears while sucking on a candy cane shamefully).

We had amazing Peruvian food after. Try La Carreta if you haven't already and try the 'ceviche' to eat and 'chicha morada' to drink. Tell them Jerry sent you and.... well, NOTHING WILL HAPPEN BECAUSE NOBODY KNOWS ME THERE! 😭 (runs away a little further while wailing in agony).

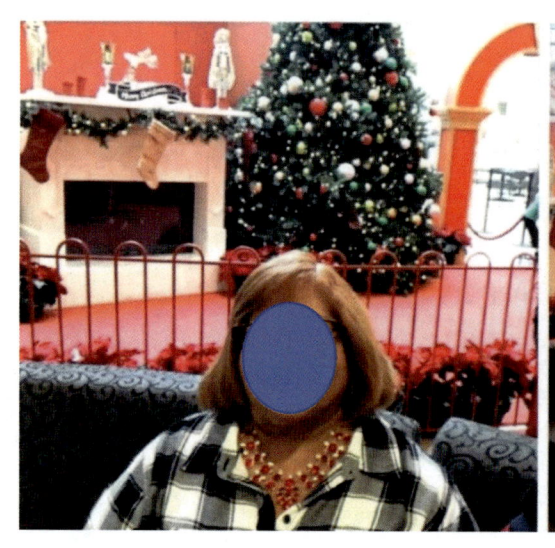

156

Here's the latest on my so-called life: I was asked to perform for non other than Beyoncé and Jay Z. I managed to set up their VIP rooms, but I'll miss the concert at because I have medical leave due to an injury to the head. I lost my balance and almost fainted due to not eating well and stress. 15 stitches! That was painful! Of course, I don't remember anything about last night but paramedics informed me of the incident. I was so pissed! Not because I have this new scar now but simply because I didn't get it as a result of something better like wrestling a burglar or fighting a bear off a helpless child. Nope... my nemesis was none other than hypoglycemia! Lol.

I got to meet someone semi-famous, I guess. So apparently the concert is tomorrow. Lol. I prepared a room for Chloe and Halley B. I immediately thought of Chloe Kardashian and Halle Berry. I got SO excited about Halley I was ready with a Catwoman joke. Then I see these two teenage girls walking along side holding hands around some people because they wanted to see their dressing room. It looked like a scene from The Shining. Someone said "I think that's Chloe and Halley". I "corrected" the guy saying "no, those look like two burn victims from, I'm guessing, the Make a Wish Foundation" thinking Beyoncé was their wish. Then they told me these two porcelain dolls-looking tweens were an up and coming R&B singing group who were the opening act for the concert. The "B" stands for Halley Bailey. Seriously!!!??? All I did was break my back, walk miles and miles around that huge stadium and carry heavy crap in the hot weather all day from noon to 8pm only to not make the concert because I can't remember to eat at times due to stress! Ugh! I was REALLY looking forward to meet Beyoncé 😔

Live each day of your life as if it was your last because that way you will appreciate every single moment. Better yet, live each day of your life as if it was your first because then every day can be the beginning of a new journey. Whether you live each day as it's your first or your last you should probably have a diaper on. - Ellen Degeneres

I love your crazy religion. Virgin births, water turns to wine, fish multiply, shrubbery talks to you... It's like Harry Potter, but with genocide, bad folk music and the constant subconscious believe that you are better than others

The things I do for a pretty face! I took the bus and sat next to the cutest guy from Switzerland. We had such a great conversation that I actually ended up stopping much further than I needed to just to keep talking to him. Had to walk almost 2 1/2 unnecessary miles back home. TOTALLY worth it! Lol

♦

What do we want?!

BETTER AUTO-CORRECT ON OUR PHONES!!!

When do we want it?!

MEOW...! BROW...! Damn it!!!! COW! F#% This!

Marilyn

Marilyn Monroe was a very beautiful and misunderstood actress. Her legacy of movies and way of being will be with us for generations! No one thought of her as the smart individual she truly was because the world casted her as a brainless sex symbol. In reality, Marilyn was truly gifted and quick-witted. She had talent for comedy and could charm the pants of every reporter with her sarcasm and double entendre. Here are some mentionable quotes from this very smart and talented woman.

"SOMETIMES YOU JUST HAVE TO THROW ON A CROWN AND REMIND THEM WHO THEY'RE DEALING WITH."

Women who see to be equal with men lack ambition

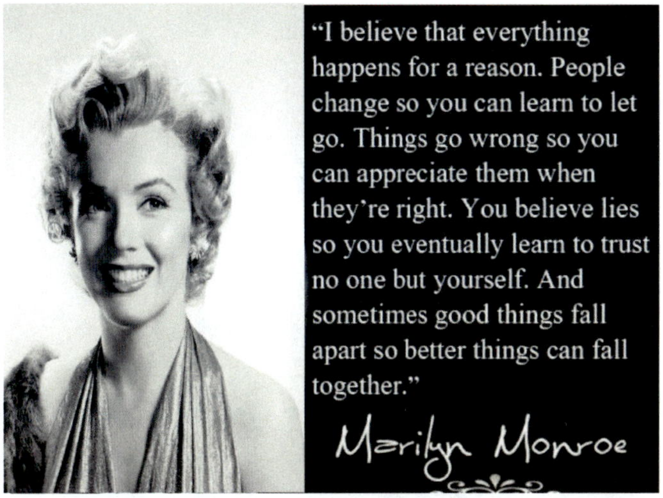

"I believe that everything happens for a reason. People change so you can learn to let go. Things go wrong so you can appreciate them when they're right. You believe lies so you eventually learn to trust no one but yourself. And sometimes good things fall apart so better things can fall together."
— Marilyn Monroe

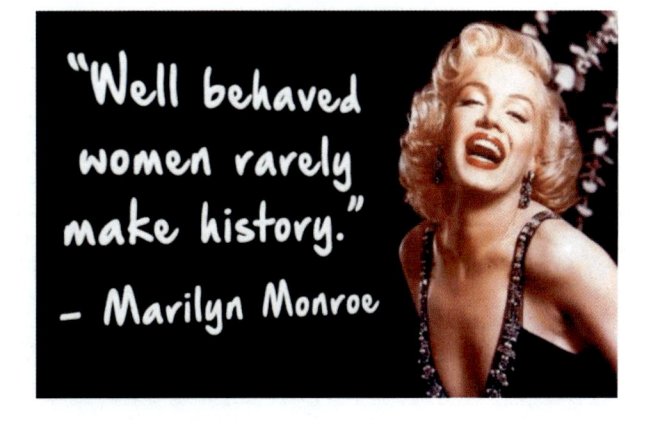

"Well behaved women rarely make history."
— Marilyn Monroe

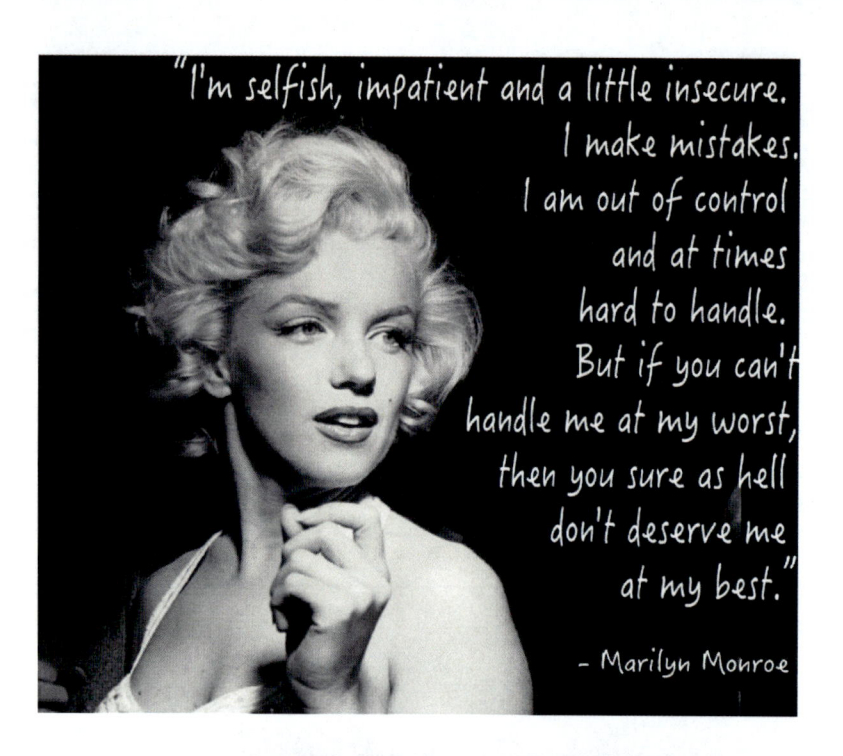

"I'm selfish, impatient and a little insecure. I make mistakes. I am out of control and at times hard to handle. But if you can't handle me at my worst, then you sure as hell don't deserve me at my best."

- Marilyn Monroe

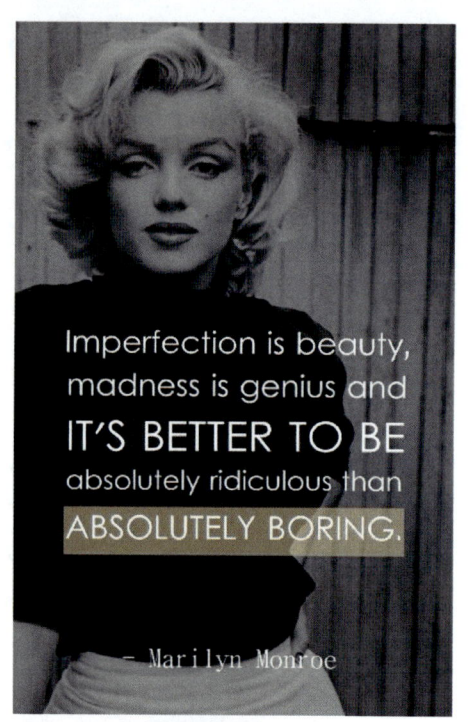

Imperfection is beauty, madness is genius and IT'S BETTER TO BE absolutely ridiculous than ABSOLUTELY BORING.

- Marilyn Monroe

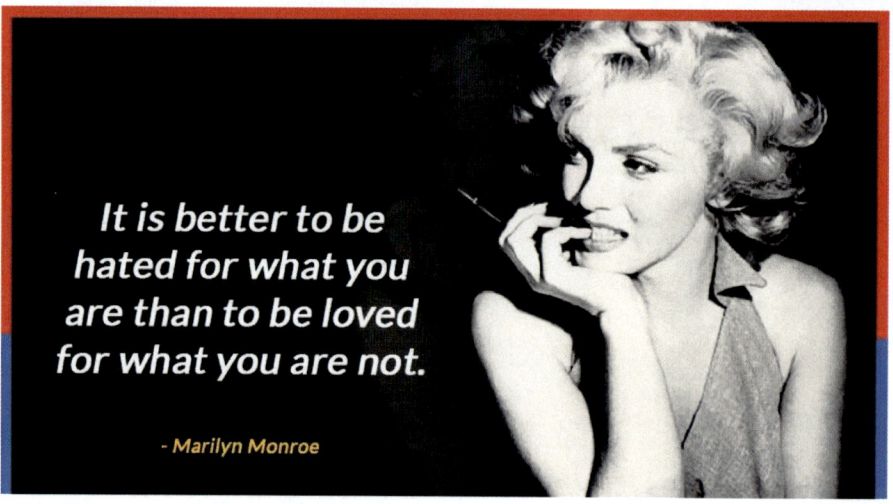

It is better to be hated for what you are than to be loved for what you are not.

- Marilyn Monroe

I don't mind living in a man's world, as long as I can be a WOMAN in it.

"Sweetie, if you're going to be two faced, at least make one of them pretty"

-Marilyn Monroe

The Wonders of Text Messaging

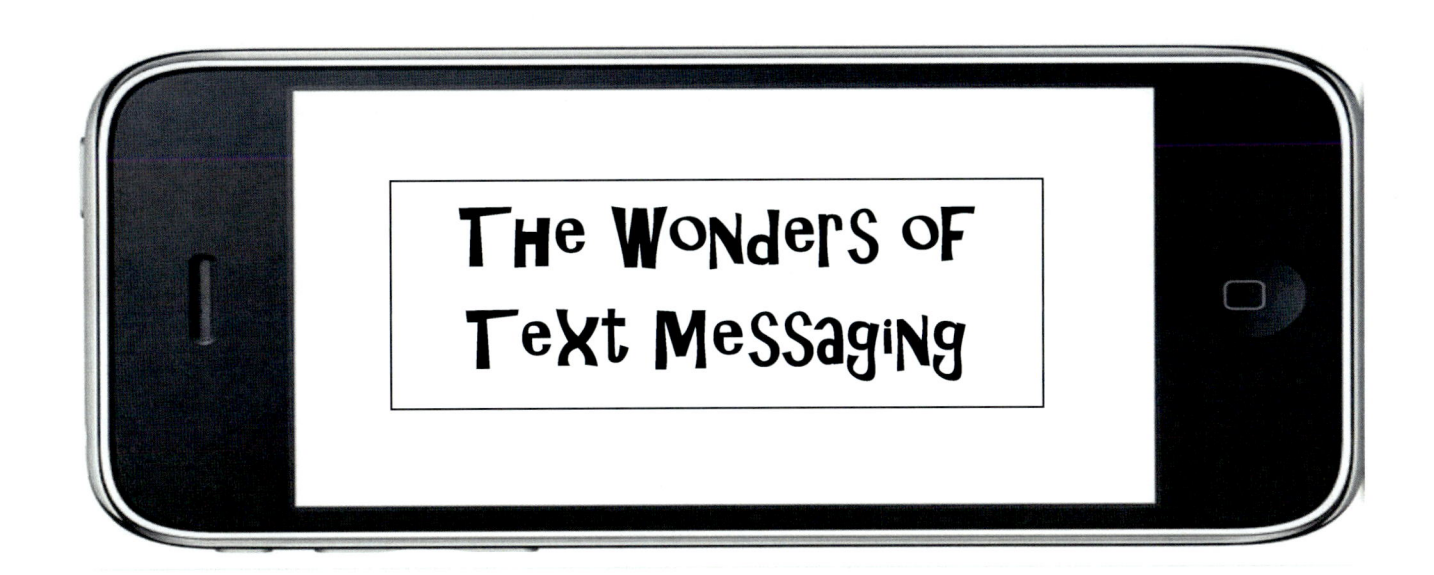

(My responses are in **BLUE**)

Come on! I promise you'll have a good time!
I'd really like to believe you, but I've already met you.

My friend and I are always coming up with rude remarks
(or "burns") we say to each other as a joke:
Buddy, your sense of humor is the gift that keeps on…being returned as a reminder to always keep our receipts when we go shopping. I'm just kidding about your humor being bad...said no one ever. Anyway, would you like to come to the art gallery with me?!
Are you kidding?! I'd love to spend hours and hours at the art gallery with you…said no one ever.
By the way…Have you been working out? Wait, let me answer that for you. You have not. You look like sh*t. Ha ha! I'm just kidding! You look amazing.... said no one ever.

Why do you hate Twilight® so much?!
I'd love to read the series, but I have this damn good taste for good literary work that keeps me from doing that! Damn you, good taste! Damn you to hell!
You're just saying that because you haven't given it a chance.
You're killing me with this conversation.
Reading the books is a lot different than watching the movies…
That's it…I'm dying. I can feel it now.
… it's so much more suspenseful and erotic…
There's the bright light. I see it now. I'm coming, Jesus!
… the action scenes just keep you on edge with every word…
Rosebud…!

Wait, they don't know we know?
They don't know that we know, but they think we know what they already know, so as long as no one says that we know what they already know, then no one will know.
You know what? I hate you.

I found a pregnancy test. Would you like to know if you're pregnant?
Don't you have to have sex first before getting pregnant?
Are you forgetting what happened last month with that guy you told me about?
Oh yeah, I should give him a call. He was fun. What was his name again?
I think it was something like John or Josh...
(Another friend of ours yells at us from across the room) You're a man! You can't get pregnant because you're a man!
So…does that mean we're not doing this anymore?
Oh…no, we totally are! You can never be too sure.

A telemarketer had just texted me about wanting to sell me a different phone plan. I said I wasn't interested many times before and blocked the number, but they just kept finding ways to reach out to me!
I've already told you I am not interested and advised you to put me on a DO NOT CALL list. I am 2 seconds away from reporting you to the Better Business Bureau. DO NOT CALL ME! DO NOT TEXT ME! And if you knock on my door causing me a heart attack from fright, DO NOT RESUSITATE!

Happy Wrapping Wednesday! (I got this text on December 23rd)
What do you mean "wrapping Wednesday?" For Throwback Thursdays I'm required to share baby pictures with a bunch of strangers and now what?, So, do I grab a condom and wrap up my meat when I'm in heat? (Hey, that rhymed!) Or should I start wrapping Christmas presents today? I don't have time for that, biotch! You come here and wrap my presents and you and your boyfriend can come to my house and bend over for "f*ck you Fridays"! Now everyone has a thing to do every day of the freaking week just because the activity starts with the same damn letter of the f*cking alphabet?! On top of that, I have my aunt who sends me messages like "have a happy Monday" or "blessed Tuesday", or "miraculous Wednesday", etc. EVERY F*CKING DAY OF THE WEEK, EVERY WEEK OF EVERY MONTH! WTF?! Those don't even rhyme, dumb ass! Screw-your-internet Saturdays is what I'm wishing for her! So yeah, I'm not wrapping sh*t. You wrap sh*t or eat a wrap or listen to rap which is not written the same way, but it sounds the same. Man! Now you got me making no sense!
Geez! Have you had your coffee today?
Yeah, so?
Please, for the sake of humanity…try decaf!

What's up? (Someone texted me this at 3am)
The sky, the clouds and my stress levels when people ask me "what's up?" at 3 am!

Random Conversations with Random People Chosen at Random (By the way, my responses are in red)

I was talking to my sister about different types of painful experiences. I told her there is no greater pain than getting your "thingy" stuck in a zipper. She tells me I would not think that way if I was a mother because there is no greater pain than childbirth. I said:
"We get our junk stuck in a zipper once in our lives and we are forever careful from that moment on and reminded of that horrible experience every time we zip up our pants. You had your 'painful experience' happen two more times BY CHOICE, so I win!"
She didn't seem to like my answer.
"Did I tell you how much I love those kids?!"

My friend had just complimented me on a joke I told him. "You're funny" – he types. This is my LONG response:

No, YOU'RE funny!
Ok, now you're supposed to say: "no, no...YOU'RE the funny one"
And then I say: "Bruh! No, no, no...YOU'RE hilarious".
Then you respond: "Daaaaaling! YOU'RE the hilarious one!" (You speak this way because of your British accent even though you're Scottish, you traitor!)
Then I respond back: "Papi, YOU'RE too much!" (Because of my Latino accent).
Then you say: "Shut up! I won't hear another word! You, my friend are amazing!"
Then I'll say: "Don't tell me to shut up, you stupid Scottish Fag-pipe! (Get it? It's like 'bagpipe', but you're a blatant homosexual and I'm a comedic genius).
Then you say: "Don't call me that, you miniature Chalupa"! (Even though I'm not Mexican)
Then I say: "Why don't you go clean my Batcave, Alfred"! (You know, 'cause you're older than me and I'm younger and prettier).
Then you say: "Why don't you go, clean my kitchen, Rosario!" (Because it sounds like a Latina maid's name, you racist bastard!)
Then I say: "Take that back, you British concubine!" (OK, I would've called you a 'slut', but hearing your British accent makes me feel proper and so pretty).

Then you say you won't take it back, so I pull out a pen from my pocket and you pull out a pack of gum (it's all we were carrying at the time) and we battle it out. But wait! Did I mention my pen is one of those needle-like pointy fountain pens? "A HA! KAPOW, Bitch! I got you now! I should celebrate by dropping the mic, but since I don't have a mic, I'm going to drop my pen on the floor. PEN DROP, bitch!"

Uh oh.... I'm disarmed now. Then you choke me and I die.

The End

OMG! You're so random! I'm literally laughing my ass off right now! LOL

Am wondering, anyone see what I see, it's a mountain see the man walking, but besides that what do you see?

A friend of mine was telling me about his divorce and how pissed off he was about having gone through so many horrible experiences with this man:
Let's play a movie trivia game. I'm going to pretend to be watching a movie and you have to tell me what I'm watching.
Let's do it!
OK, uh… Don't go in the water. It's gonna kill you!
Uh… Swamp Thing?
No, it's gonna kill you because of its huge sharp teeth. If you go fishing, you're gonna need a bigger boat!
Jaws! LOL
Good job! Ok, here's another one… Don't do it! You'll regret it!
Uh… any mafia movie there is? I don't know…
No! Don't go inside that church! He's waiting for you there to make your life a living hell?!
I give up.
I'm watching your wedding video.
LOL. This is the first time I talk about my wedding with that jerk and laugh about it.

Random Randomness
(My responses will now be in green because I'm a chameleon)

Hope you had a nice day. Mine was pretty decent. Nothing out of the ordinary. You know...the usual... went shopping with Britney Spears, naked mud wrestling with Chris Pratt, Chris Hemsworth and Chris Evans (it was a dirty Chris-tening. Get it? Uh? (Nods you with elbow) & finally went swimming with the sharks. At least I think they were sharks. They were all wearing their protective surgical masks, so I didn't get to see their jaws. They could've just been dolphins playing the Jaws theme song very loudly on their portable stereo to appear more menacing. Who knows?

What are you up to?
Yay! I'm jumping up and down...on a trampoline.... Woohoo! Yippie! My tits are bouncing...some guys just stopped by to watch and are now recording me with their camera phones....
...
...
...

I'm getting off this trampoline.

What are you up to?
Not much. Just having a normal day. You know, playing crochet with the Queen of England, taking cooking lessons with Martha Stewart and later I'm gonna crash a wedding to make the bride trip as she walks down the aisle. Hey! We all need a hobby.

What's up?
Not much. I walked into a room and yelled out "I'm a top"! The next thing I saw was a stampede of guys running towards me looking like footage taken from a store during Black Friday as they opened their doors to the public early in the morning!

How was your day?

- Well, I managed to get out of bed, get dressed and put on the same type of shoe on each foot, so I would say I'm having a pretty good day.

- You know, the usual… I was asked to judge a cock-fight in Habana and then I jumped off a plane, but I didn't have a parachute, so I had to rely on my bedsheets to do the trick. After landing, I performed open-heart surgery on an extinct baby Bald Eagle.

- Nothing out of the ordinary. Saved a baby carriage from an upcoming train to then realize it was empty. It was just a distraction to allow these guys to rob a bank, but I was able to stop them before the authorities came with backup.
  Oh my God! REALLY?!
  Nah, just gave birth to triplets.

What do you mean you don't think you're anyone's type?!
Well, I'm pushy, creative, indecisive, dramatic, passionate, opinionated, anxious... Basically, I need a man whose dream is to marry a nightmare!

A friend of mine was suggesting I waited for the following day to buy a bottle of lubricant for…uh…a thing. I told him that I was sure I would be able to find an alternative to that somewhere in the house. Thirty minutes later, I sent him this message:

Holy mother of mercy! You know I never learn a lesson because someone just told me to do the right thing. I have to plummet headfirst into a mistake for me to learn something from the experience. So, I tried this blue gel designed ONLY for sore muscles and it was not what I expected.

I must say that at first was kind of nice because it was the first time that he felt cold, but he was also getting bigger instead of smaller. Yes, I said "he". My thing has a persona and its own name: Scrappy Doodle Perez Santiago. So, it started out all slippery and icy hot and then burned like hell! It was like getting a handjob from Satan after him juggling hot lava rocks at the circus!

MY GOD! I AM SO BORED HERE!!! Don't be surprised if I come back to Florida as a woman because I was so bored, I decided to have a sex change just for the hell of it. Then Scrappy will have to change its name to Maria Rosario Rodriguez Beaverhousen the 3rd.

A friend of mine was asking me about the gay guys in Puerto Rico and what their sexual preferences were compared to those from the ones living in Central Florida.
You know what? It seems like everyone here is a top. Not like back in FL. Back there you say "I'm a top" and guys come rushing towards you making it look like footage taken from a stampede in Africa. Gotta love Whore-lando. I hear it's the same way in Fort Bottom-dale. (referring to Orlando and Fort Lauderdale).

A friend of mine was complaining that he was not lucky finding girls who would be interested to go out with him on a date…
Personally, I think you're a good-looking guy. So…seriously, what's wrong with you? Are you a serial murderer? Do you think recycling is stupid? Are you a Satanist? You into cannibalism? Do you not use your turning signals when driving?
"LOL. It's cool. I know I will eventually meet someone when I least expect it".
I agree, but seriously though…. Do you have a third nipple? Do you not return your books from the library on time? Do you go to people's houses uninvited to ask them if they've accepted Jesus Christ as their savior? Do you wear white after Labor Day? Do you leave the toilet seat up after use? You a cellphone user while the movie plays in the theater? What is it?! TELL ME?!!!!!!

When you die but your cats still want to meow at you at 3AM for food

Undress me with your words Darling

There's a spider in your bra

When you're dyslexic and accidentally write to satan instead of santa

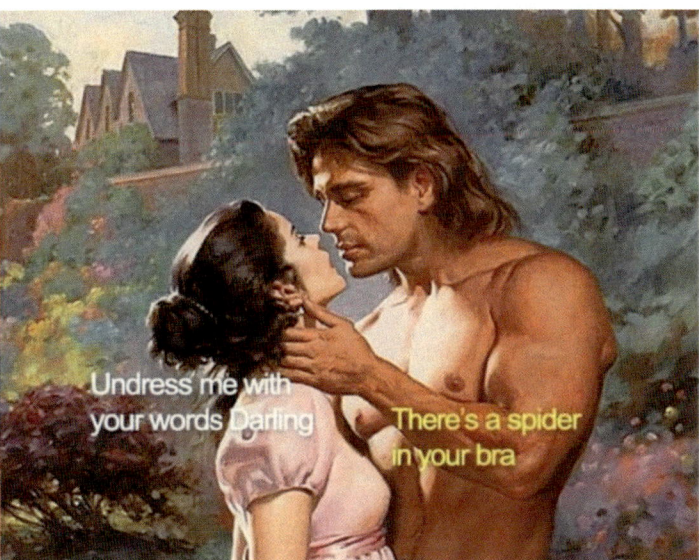

Jesus walks into a bar: "Just 12 waters please!" *winks at disciples*

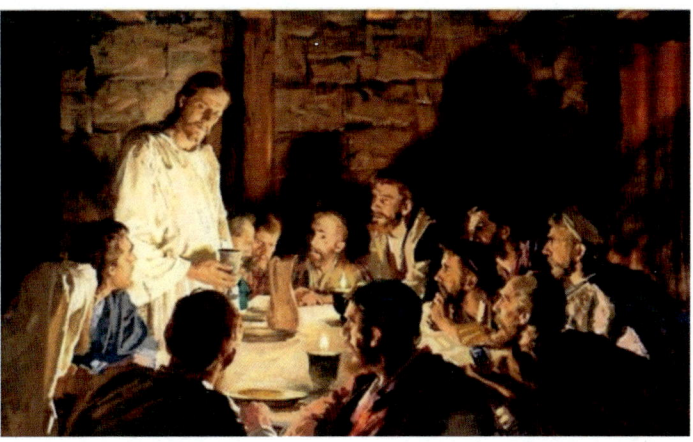

"We aren't falling for it again, Gary, we know your dong is in the fruit"

"Earth" without "art" is just "Eh"

MEME Time!

Every time I'm asked to babysit for my sister, and she asks how the baby (or as we call him "chubs" or "the chubster" because of his cute belly) is doing, I send her one of these...

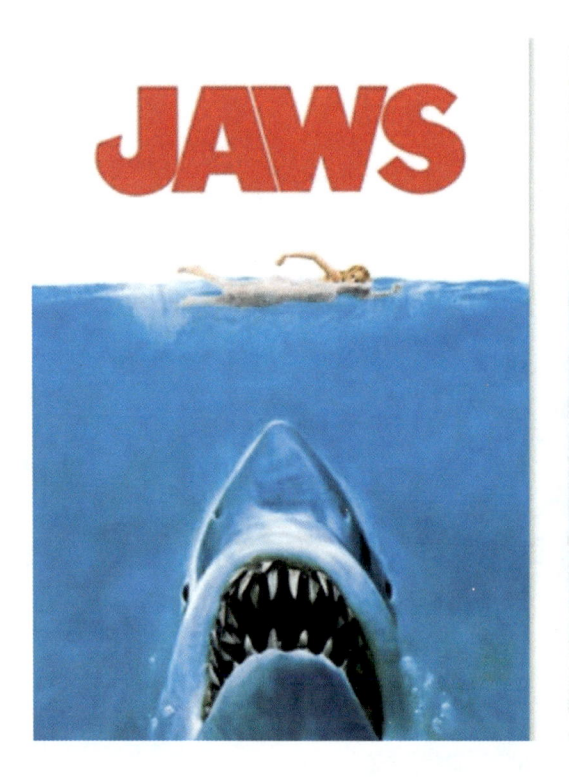

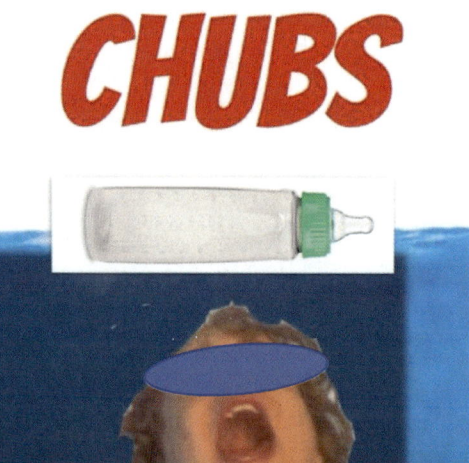

JAWS

CHUBS

Wolver-chubs

BEETLECHUBS!!!

168

"We meet again, Catwoman"

WHO WORE IT BETTER?

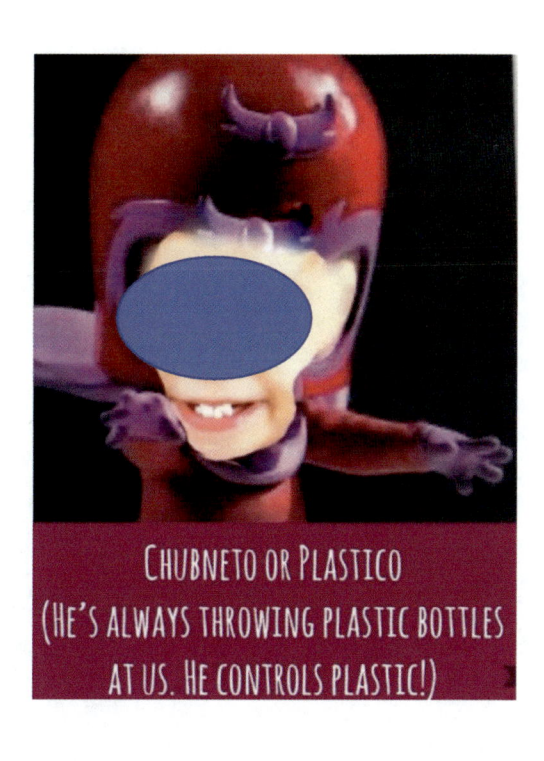

Chubneto or Plastico
(He's always throwing plastic bottles at us. He controls plastic!)

Pica-chubs

169

They may take away my pants, but they'll never take away MY CHEETOS!

You are not gonna believe what I heard about the neighbor!

#babygossip

I DON'T KNOW

QUICK, LOOK IN HERE!

Where's the turkey I left here?

JUGGER-CHUBS

So full of hopes & dreams
1
2
3
Soul crushed forever 😔
REALITY!!!

BEWARE OF LITTLE MONSTERS

Crap! They know I'm here?!

Disney has to be basing their characters on my family album!

Who wore it better? 🤔

PIC·COLLAGE

Baby Yoda

The whole "baby Yoda craze" was insane! Everybody wanted one, his picture was everywhere and that's all people talked about in social media. There were SO MANY "memes" created, it was sickening! So, anyway...
here are some more I came up with!

Me: What do you mean I can't beat him?! How tall is he? I'll show you, damn it! Where is that piece of...?"

Also me: Uh...

SOMEONE THREW A BOTTLE OF MAYO AT ME

I WAS LIKE "WHAT THE HELLMANN"

(This one's not mine)

Older people always poked me at weddings and said "you're next"

So, I started doing the same thing to them at funerals

At the restaurant or coffee shop...

ME: Hi, may I please order a pumpkin-flavored...
THEM: I'm sorry, we stopped serving those last season.
ALSO ME....

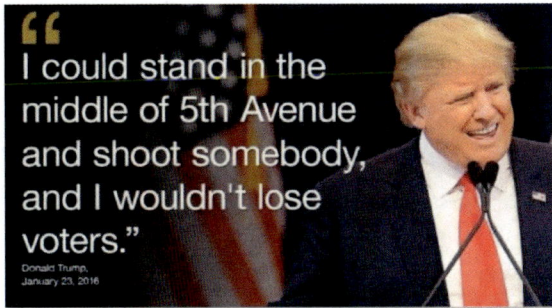

"I could stand in the middle of 5th Avenue and shoot somebody, and I wouldn't lose voters."
Donald Trump, January 23, 2016

Jerry Perez
5d · Lolsided

This is SO true! I just tell the staff to let me borrow the cheese grater and I'll give it back when I'm finished (A.K.A. when there's no more cheese left)

Jerry refusing to say "when" while the waiter covers his dish with cheese:

(This one's not mine)

173

When you tell a joke, but nobody laughs

Then you hear someone else repeating it and everybody laughs

WHAT THEY SAY AT SOME OF THE WORST RESTAURANTS EVER!:
"We're sorry, sir. We stopped serving breakfast at 10:30am"

ME: But...

I heard Chris Hemsworth uses this particular bathroom stall at exactly 3pm

Me at 2:28pm:

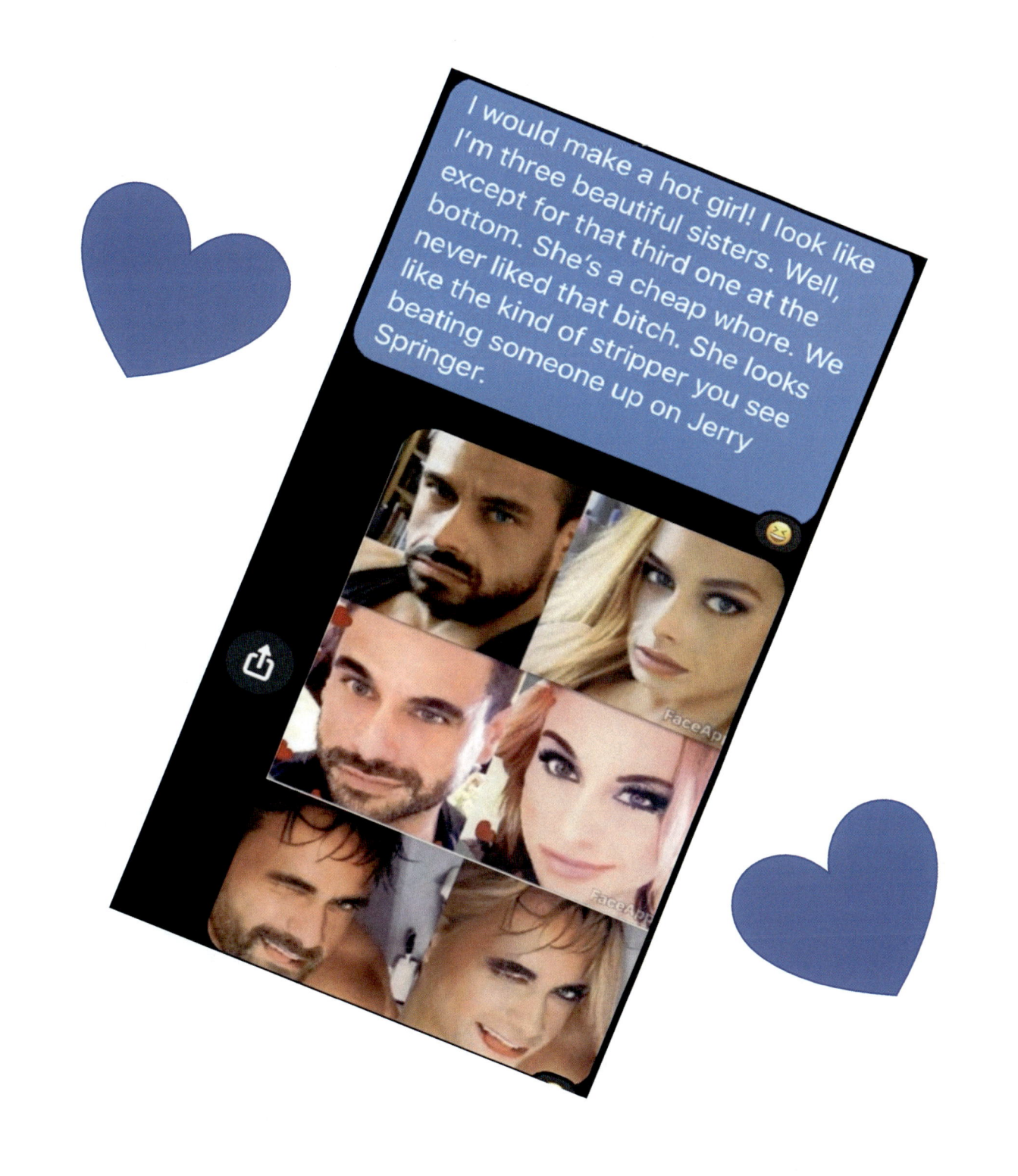

> I would make a hot girl! I look like I'm three beautiful sisters. Well, except for that third one at the bottom. She's a cheap whore. We never liked that bitch. She looks like the kind of stripper you see beating someone up on Jerry Springer.

Love

Poetry

I started a new diet and
I've been feeling pretty good,
but who the hell would start it
before eating so much food?!

Thanksgiving dinner was just great
and we had turkey, bread and yams.
But the "Monkey Cake" prepared
was, by far, dinner's star.

I tried a piece just to taste it
and then I could not stop!
Cinnamon, Nutella and brown sugar
made my little heart stop.

I will be hiding for a while
in sweat pants by the patio.
I'll be working on my tan
and 50 hours of cardio!

I like to wear Batman® shirts,
but I really don't know why.
I go to work and shower every day
so I'm a normal kind of guy.

My Obssesion

I bought a nice black face mask
and wore it the other day.
I thought my friends would like it,
but instead they walked away.

I'd like to dress as Batman.
I would do it every day!
The hardest thing about that
would be explaining that on dates.

I wish I was as heroic, calculating,
more cunning and more brash.
But what I really envy of him
are his butler and the cash.

But there is more than geeky clothes
I want to see when I look in the mirror.
I'll work hard and make the world proud
as I live my life as someone's hero!

iDicted

I wake up in the morning
with the buzzing of my alarm
that, thanks to my iPhone,
I can easily disarm.

But the fun doesn't stop there
and I think I'm greatly in love;
and today I'm not afraid to share
that I am nothing without my smart-phone.

Right after I wake up, it reminds me
of emails to answer and things to do.
It also tells me about the weather
right after I have read the news.
I know I could read a paper
or see that on TV,
but I still think my way is better
'cuz no one is smarter than me.

I can scan just about anything
like products and specials
to find the best restaurant
or get a free facial.
I can buy what I want
from a theater ticket to a movie.
I know there are stores for that,
but isn't this way kinda' groovy?

I track my gym workouts,
what I eat and where I go.
I play videos and music
while I do my cardio.
I can also get distracted
with an iBook or a game.
I know there's friends for that,
but this way is less lame.

Speaking of friends,
you know I got plenty:
Facebook, My Space,
Tumblr, Twitter...
I could delete those,
But ma' raised no quitter.

I can take and edit photos
and it tells me where to go.
I can pay every single bill
and keep my stocks and bonds.
If I need reminders,
I got a calendar for that
and I could never tip a waiter right,
if I didn't have that App.
I know I could learn
directions, art or math,
but I'm about to read my horoscope
so I ain't got time for that.

Now the day is finally over
and I'm thinking of tomorrow with anticipation.
I set my alarm after brushing my teeth
while getting more and more applications.
I go to bed feeling accomplished
and my day sure was fun,
but ask me how many people I talked to…
I'm afraid the answer is "none".

Crazy Cat Carlitos

My name is Carlitos.
I'm a cat who is "chiquito".
And I drink my Hornitos®
while I eat my burrito.

I'm working on an essay
titled "What's Up, Ese?"
Where I talk about the headaches
I get from _____
        (insert word that rhymes with
        "headaches". What do you
        want from me?! I'm just a cat
        after all! It's a miracle I was able
        to type all of this so far!)

I'm gonna dance to bachata
and eat lots of frittata.
I'm gonna break a piñata
'cause it's my birthday mañana!

Look at Me!

I try to get your attention
in a hundred different ways.
You only put me in detention
and miss my gaze again!

I poop on the rug,
I poop on the sofa.
I poop on your mug
while you do yoga.
I poop on your floor.
I poop on your laundry
I poop near your door
and your food when you're hungry.
I poop on... are you gonna take me out for a walk or what?!!!

Fried Love

The rumors are true.
You can smell it on my apron.
I must break up with you
because I rather be with bacon.

Bacon is toasty.
Bacon is rough.
One strip of bacon
is never enough!

Oh sweet greasy lover!
Give me a honey-roasted kiss.
Make me swoon and my heart flutter.
You are heaven…you are bliss!

Mother Spellcheck

Spellcheck is starting to remind me of mom.
This assumption is very recent.
She's always correcting the way that I talk
and tries to make me look decent.

When I type "shit",
I'm encouraged to "shoot"
and squeeze a "book's" pages
when I rather squeeze "boobs".

Birds have more fun
when I say I am "fucking"
because, like it or not,
my phone says I'm "ducking".

"Dick" is turned to a "Duck".
I get "cocktails" when I want "Cock".
Will I speak without using curse words?
I think that ship has sailed, dear mom.

My $ecret Love

You raise me up when I am down.
You smell like the freshest flowers!
There are no frowns when you're around.
You combine beauty and power.

Words cannot describe
How happy you make me.
I know glory has arrived
and joy is now alive
in my life that was so empty.

When you're not around
I get so, so sad.
I can't get around
or buy what I want.

You're my love, my angel
My sugar and honey.
You're my jewel, my treasure.
Man! I love money!

WHY ENGLISH IS HARD TO LEARN

We'll begin with *box*; the plural is *boxes*,
But the plural of ox is *oxen*, not *oxes*.
One fowl is a *goose*, and two are called *geese*,
Yet the plural of *moose* is never called *meese*.

You may find a lone *mouse* or a house full of *mice*;
But the plural of *house* is *houses*, not *hice*.
The plural of *man* is always *men*,
But the plural of *pan* is never *pen*.

If I speak of a *foot*, and you show me two *feet*,
And I give you a *book*, would a pair be a *beek*?
If one is a *tooth* and a whole set are *teeth*,
Why shouldn't two *booths* be called *beeth*?

If the singular's *this* and the plural is *these*,
Should the plural of *kiss* be ever called *keese*?

We speak of a *brother* and also of *brethren*,
But though we say *mother*, we never say *methren*.
Then the masculine pronouns are *he*, *his*, and *him*;
But imagine the feminine . . . *she*, *shis*, and *shim*!

Simply Papers

(I wrote this poem to gift to my mother on Christmas Day)

What do you gift the woman who has it all?
Today I humbly gift my words,
but tomorrow you'll have more.
Today I only have papers... simply papers...

nothing more.

God has given me a gift
that not many get to enjoy.
And as silly as this sounds,
I gift you papers... simply papers...

nothing more.

But papers are important
from the moment we are born.
Our birth certificate is just a paper...
simply a paper...

nothing more.

We learn a lot in school.
Many lessons come and go,
but for these to be remembered
we write them in papers... simply papers...

nothing more.

We see unforgettable movies
and go to plays a lot.
These, plane tickets, theme parks...
will require papers...simply papers...

nothing more.

We couldn't be more excited
as we enter our first home,
but it needs to be remodeled.
Deeds are papers... simply papers...

nothing more.

We work for a living, make friends
and fall in love.
A million poems are written on papers...
simply papers...

nothing more.

We're invited to many events
and meet friends and family as we go.
One day we get married and sign a certificate
on a piece of paper...simply a paper...

nothing more.

We grow older and one day
declared deceased on a form.
Millions will gather to tell stories about us
that they've written on papers... simply papers...

nothing more.

I wish I could gift you the moon, the stars, the sun
for all the years you've made me happy.
I hope this poem and these flowers you enjoy
even if they are papers... simply papers...

nothing more.

(I learned how to make paper flowers and surrounded my mother with different arrangements. Each one represented a special moment in our lives together as a family. Because she only knows Spanish, I translated and framed the poem for her. All the flowers had a different scent. I used body spray for this effect)

Papeles

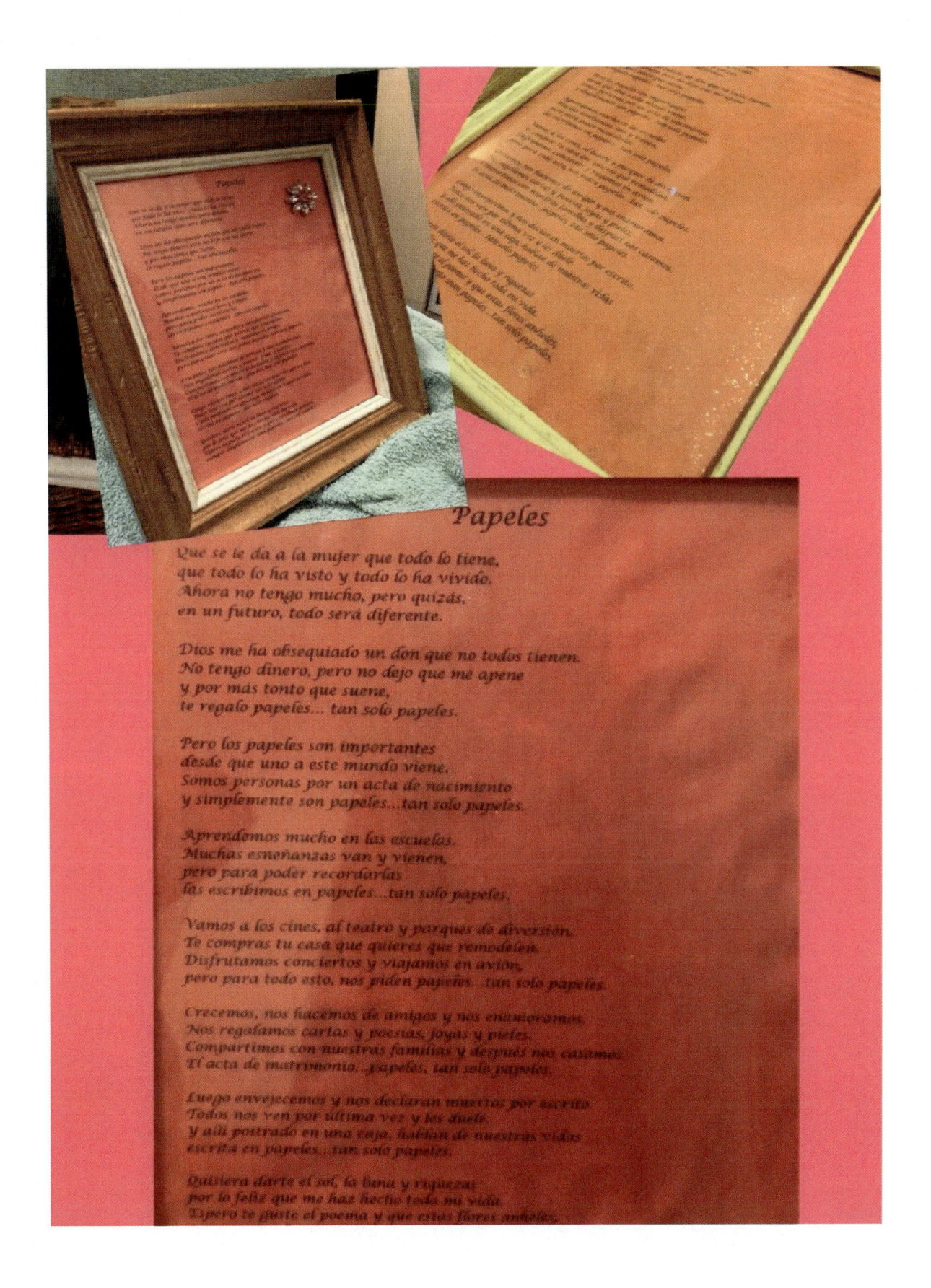

Qué se le da a la mujer que todo lo tiene,
que todo lo ha visto y todo lo ha vivido.
Ahora no tengo mucho, pero quizás,
en un futuro, todo será diferente.

Dios me ha obsequiado un don que no todos tienen.
No tengo dinero, pero no dejo que me apene
y por más tonto que suene,
te regalo papeles... tan solo papeles.

Pero los papeles son importantes
desde que uno a este mundo viene.
Somos personas por un acta de nacimiento
y simplemente son papeles...tan solo papeles.

Aprendemos mucho en las escuelas.
Muchas eseñanzas van y vienen,
pero para poder recordarlas
las escribimos en papeles...tan solo papeles.

Vamos a los cines, al teatro y parques de diversión.
Te compras tu casa que quieres que remodelen.
Disfrutamos conciertos y viajamos en avión,
pero para todo esto, nos piden papeles...tan solo papeles.

Crecemos, nos hacemos de amigos y nos enamoramos.
Nos regalamos cartas y poesías, joyas y pieles.
Compartimos con nuestras familias y después nos casamos.
El acta de matrimonio...papeles, tan solo papeles.

Luego envejecemos y nos declaran muertos por escrito.
Todos nos ven por última vez y les duele
Y allí postrado en una caja, hablan de nuestras vidas
escrita en papeles...tan solo papeles.

Quisiera darte el sol, la luna y riquezas,
por lo feliz que me has hecho toda mi vida.
Espero te guste el poema y que estas flores anheles,

These flowers represent the many Holidays we spent together as a family

Estas flores representan las navidades que pasamos en familia. La música, los bailes, la comida, los alborotos, el ruido, las tradiciones... momentos de caótica belleza.

These flowers are all different and stand for the many lives she touched or saved

Estas flores son todas diferentes y representan las vidas de tantas personas que has impactado. Has salvado vidas y has ayudado a mucha gente a sobresalir, incluyéndome a mí. Gracias por siempre estar ahí para asegurarte que estuviera bien. He regalado muchas flores en mi vida, pero las flores cambian con el tiempo y se marchitan. Esta es la primera vez que intento imitar algo que Dios nos ha obsequiado en la naturaleza. Pero estas nunca cambiarán, nunca se van a marchitar. Estas flores representan el amor que tengo por ti, porque éste nunca morirá.

These flowers represent her support for my art. She planted the seed and watered it grow

Esta flor representa mi arte y el apoyo que siempre me has brindado para forjarlo. Me hiciste estudiar mucho y esto siempre te lo voy a agradecer. Tan pronto viste mi deseo por escribir a una tierna edad, me regalaste una máquina de escribir y así te convertiste en la fanática más grande que tengo. Gracias por sembrar esa semilla que es mi arte y verla crecer.

These flowers represent my mother, my sister, my grandmother and my niece

No tengo muchos recuerdos en mi mente, pero le doy gracias a Dios por haberme concedido retener unos de los más bellos. Los recuerdos son muy importantes para mí y pensé que en esta Navidad podría regalarte lo que yo más anhelo en este mundo... lo más que me entristece haber perdido años atrás... quiero regalarte este momento que espero recuerdes por ambos toda la vida. Gracias por ser una madre tan ejemplar y perfecta. Eres la flor más linda de mi jardín. Las mujeres de nuestra familia son un ejemplo de amor, sacrificios, ternura y prosperidad que, lamentablemente, no muchas tienen la dicha de tener. Estas flores te representan a ti, a mi Lelita cariñosa, a mi hermana tan fiel y a mi sobrina tan bella que son lo más dulce que Dios ha puesto en esta tierra!

These flowers represent our childhood. She made us Raggedy Ann and Raggedy Andy® costumes for our first Halloween and we visited the Disney® parks every year

Nuestra niñez fué perfecta. Tu fuiste el guardian de nuestras fantasias. Gracias a ti, nos acostábamos temprano en navidad para ver los regalos que Santa Claus nos dejo. Poniamos los dientes que perdimos al crecer bajo nuestras almohadas con la esperanza de ser premiados con monedas mágicas. Nuestras vacaciones a Disney World nos enseñaron que los heroes existian y todo era posible si realmente lo deseamos. Estas flores representan nuestra niñez que, gracias a ti, estuvo llena de magia y fantasia.

193

194

So Close. Yet So Far
(About loving someone despite dealing with amnesia)

He sleeps alone in bed at night.
He is so close and yet so far.
He dreams of peace and works so hard.
I wish him well as I kiss him goodbye.

I always smile while by his side,
so he knows how happy he makes me.
I talk about him day or night...
my life without him would be so empty.

I walk around this quiet home
as I leave him to head to work.
So many memories within these walls...
and many dreams are yet to forge.

I may cry at times and things forget
because I don't have a great mind.
But his smile I'll always save
because it is engraved in my heart.

The Last Poem
(About breakups)

Every night, the sun dies a little.
Every rainbow fades away.
Every answer is wrapped in riddles.
And every day I love him less.

Heroes fight for what they love.
I've travelled miles for just one kiss.
There is no one at my door...
no one there to fight for me.

The night has a thousand eyes,
the day has none but one...
Yet the light of the whole world dies
with the agonizing sun.
The mind has a thousand dreams;
the heart has only one...
Yet all is dead around me
when love is gone.

I search for you in a corner
and hope I catch you dancing
but then I remember I'm all alone
and stop myself from crying.
I searched in my hand for a ring I used to wear
and look in the closet for things we used to share.
I look in my mind for a dream I used to dream
and look endlessly for your things which are not here.
You may have gone but your presence still roams.
I talk about my day with your picture on the wall.
And I still find you in a movie or a moment or a song.
At night I whisper "I love you" as I feel you next to me,
but it was just my soft deceiving pillow
that I held so lovingly.

To say 'goodbye' is part of life
and I say these words to you and move on ahead.
To love again is the sweet punishment
of those who loved once in excess.

But there's a light deep within me
that keeps on shining through.
And that is why on this evening
I say goodbye to you.

I hope that you are happy
with the choices you have made.
And I wish I find the thing
that will send my pain away.

I am putting my pen down
and killing what I once knew
to make a needed change now,
to give birth to something new.

I have shed my last tear
and written my last truth:
for this is the last poem
that I dedicate to you.

My Birthday Wish

As the sand fills the hourglass
and midnight draws in near,
I reminisce of seasons past
and life grants me another year.

They bring the cake in front of me.
I see their smiles in a dim lit room.
They lean in closer so they can see
the happiness I must assume.

They bring the candles in so close.
Their warmth embrace my face.
I close my eyes and their light blow;
a heart-felt wish now must be made.

I'd ask for youth, but young I've been.
I'd ask for time, that I don't need.
With undying hope I dare to dream
as I make him my birthday wish.

I'd ask for health, but that I have.
I'd ask for money to be vast.
But health and riches can't compare
to the love and times we often shared.

Life had always taken things
that I always loved so dear,
so I am a fool for dreaming this.
I wish I lied but I'm sincere.

The peace of mind I cannot buy
would have made a perfect gift.
I wish I lied and did not cry
because I rather have his kiss.

I can be strong. I know that well
and I can get my act together!
But first I'll mourn and I will dwell
on the love I've lost forever.

To work on strength and not be weak;
there will be enough time for this.
But tonight I ask to leave me be
and let him be my birthday wish.

Live!

(I'm not exactly sure where I read this, but it was a beautiful piece written in Spanish about appreciating life, so I translated it for all my readers to enjoy)

People die and everything is left behind. The plans we had, housework, the bills and financial issues with our bank, our jewelry, our home, and the car we bought to improve our status.

People die and they leave all their food in the fridge. Everything rots, our clothes stay hung in our closets.

People die and all those things that we thought were important dissolve. Life goes on and people forget about your absence and continue with their routines normally.

People die and all those big problems we thought we had are transformed into empty voids. Problems live inside of us. Things only have the energy and power we give them.

People die and the world continues to be chaotic. Our presence or absence doesn't make the slightest difference. We are small, but driven. We always forget that death is right around the corner watching us.

People die so suddenly like the blink of an eye. Your dog is put up for adoption and it will love the new owners with loyalty. Widowers remarry and fall in love again. They hold hands, go to the movies, they enjoy their lives together and forget about you.

People die and are quickly replaced at their jobs. The things that we cannot use anymore are donated or thrown in the trash.

If people accepted their own deaths with open arms as opposed to worry about it, they would live happier lives. Maybe you will dress better, use a better type of perfume today, travel more, maybe people will start dessert before dinner. Maybe we would expect less from people and be more forgiving. We would love more and appreciate nature more We would worry more about time than money. If people knew that we could leave this world any second maybe they will see that is not important to be sad about things beyond our control. We would listen to more music and dance even though we don't know how. Time flies. The moment we are born we begin an amazing and fast-paced journey 'till the end of our time. It's so fast, and yet there are those who are always in a hurry. They don't gift themselves the gift of appreciation for everything around us. Every day that passes is one day less of our lives. People die all the time little by little and a little more with every minute that passes.

Answer me this, what are we doing with the time that we have left? I invite you to reflect on this and be more proactive. Enjoy every single thing this life has to offer and enjoy every opportunity you have to be happy and to make others around you happy.

New Year's Poem

With every year's end
I take a look back
at everything I have done,
the people I've met,
the ones that I have lost.

I look at the heartbreak
and the times I was loved,
the times I was hated
and the lives I have touched.

I set new goals in life
so that my failures don't repeat
because I want to make a good example
of the life that I have lived.

I am ready to be a better man.
I am ready to receive something greater.
I am ready to fight for what I believe in.
Because Lord knows I DESERVE BETTER!

I wish you all a very happy new year!
Love, health and money for 2021!
Many blessings and no more tears.
Much love to all and to all a good night

The Pink Sheep

We are born with a little sugar in our tanks
and for this, we've hidden and suffered.
Instead of hatred, we've given thanks
to God for all we've discovered.

We reinvent ourselves like the divas we love.
We never hold grudges or turn bitter.
Our hearts will be kind, not turned into stones
with a fistful of feathers and glitter.

We learned to fight adversity from an early age.
Life can be rough, confusing and tragic.
We've mastered the arts, the world and our fate
with much faith in ourselves and believing in magic

(with much love to my LGBT community)

I'm Sorry

Coming back home to live with my mother surrounded by so many pictures of my past made me think of someone who used to be in my life. I'm sure he doesn't like me very much anymore because of all the things I did to him. I don't blame him. I can't believe I'm doing this, but I need to apologize to this person and, after you read this, you may think I'm not as nice as you thought I was.

I'm sorry for making you feel that you were never good enough. Your parents' successes casted a big shadow and I always made you think you had to work very hard to earn their love and the love of your friends. That's why I made you become a model so you could look perfect and I made you write books because it wasn't enough to just read somebody else's work. I talked you into running for student council and play sports and belong to every single group in school: drama, literature, talent shows, yearbook, volleyball team, tutoring, etc. because I made you think that being popular and fitting in to every group of people and be liked by everyone was the most important thing in life. "You have to be loved and remembered" - is what I always said to you.

You would sometimes come to me with a problem that was really hurting you and I pushed it aside with a stupid joke and I taught you how to hide your feelings behind a fake smile because, if you ignore something, it usually goes away. This left you with so many scars and I should've helped you deal with your problems instead of pretending they weren't there and that's why you never believed you could do anything on your own. You became too codependent on others, and this is why all your relationships failed. You trusted many who took advantage of you because you were so naïve and incapable of finding the solution to problems in your life by yourself.

I'm sorry for making you believe that you were not interesting enough in anyone's eyes unless you were drunk or high. Because of this, you suffered many accidents, endured jail time and many costly fees that put you and your family in a horrible financial predicament at times.

You always told everyone that your favorite holiday is Halloween, and you love wearing costumes to entertain others, but I know that the only reason why you do this is to hide behind a mask. I know you would rather have a nice Christmas surrounded by all your loved ones, but unfortunately, it was impossible because your family is scattered all over the world and you were always suffering in silence in your relationships with other men even though you were always trying to convince yourself they were perfect. I know those happy posts on social media were nothing but a cry for help. Some people don't know this about you, but when you laugh the loudest and brag endlessly about how wonderful your life is, that's when you're at your saddest and loneliest.

I'm sorry for never encouraging you to finish projects that were important to you. I constantly compared you to others and ridiculed your talents and your ideas because they were not as mature or as bright as other people's. I should've pushed you to finish these because these were important to you and now, I'm afraid that the day will come when you will be on your deathbed and wonder how your life would have been if you made YOUR dreams come true. But you may never see this happen. It may be too late for you and this is all my fault. I forced you to make other people's dreams come true and convinced you this was your purpose in life.

I killed every dream you had and aspirations and hope in others and faith in love. Made you waste your money on stupid things, and I made you think you were never as good as other people.

I know apologizing is never going to bring you back or make you want to be a better person despite all the things I said and did. But I want you to know, from the bottom of my heart, that I am truly sorry. You are a wonderful guy. You are funny, talented, kind, and beautiful. Please, don't ever forget who you are and your worth again! Even though I didn't show it at times, I love you and I always will.

The man that I'm dedicating this to and who is in almost every picture around me in this big house is me. But another ME… a younger ME. The hopeful child who believed in magic, the young adult who was so hopeful and loving. I can tell he is full of hope and love and hasn't been hurt by the cruelties the world often brings yet. He was such a happy child because laughter was present every day and magic really existed. As I cry in silence as an older man today, I look for this child in every corner, in every room. I can almost hear him laughing from a distance. I wish you were here with me today to help me live my life as happy as you lived it.

I'll Show You!

(To every ex I've ever known)

I look through many pictures and I see myself smiling or doing something to make someone laugh. But I'm alone in these photographs. "Look how smart I am!" - I say as I study and write. I learn many things: how to play musical instruments, arts & crafts, different languages...

"You're not what I'm looking for" - he says. I'm rejected. It hurts. "I'll be better, you'll see!" - is my promise.

So, I exercise and go through surgeries, change the color of my eyes, appear in modeling shoots, become objectified for the pleasure of others. "Look!" - I say once again- "Look how beautiful I am!"

"You're not what I'm looking for" - he says. I'm rejected again. It hurts a bit more. "I'll be better, you'll see!" - I promise again.

I wasn't fun enough, so I enter their world of clubbing incessantly, drinks, drugs, sex... no rock n' roll. It brought me a lot of trouble and my family suffered alongside, "Hey! Look how fun I am!" - I say - "Look at me! Somebody please, look at me!"

"You're not what we're looking for" - they say to me. I am rejected a hundred times more and it hurts a lot. "I'll be better, you'll see!" - I promise yet again!

But then I take some time to think. I look at all these pictures of that insecure and lonely boy and decide it's time to stop making promises to others. Why am I constantly trying to be with someone as opposed to becoming the man anyone would feel lucky to be with? Why try to fit in if I was born to stand out? I'm lucky to have friends who remind me of my worth and a family that doesn't give up on me no matter how many mistakes I've made in my life. These people have faith in me because they know what I can do, the things I've done or accomplished and how far I have gone.

I like myself and I couldn't be happier with this realization. I am not a "boy" anymore. I am a man who is smart, handsome and fun. I want to make the world laugh beside me and I want to love and be loved and admired and remembered.

Today I look in the mirror and say to myself:

"You are EXACTLY what I'm looking for, but there's always room for improvement".

"I'll be better" - I say to <u>myself</u>...

"You'll see!"

LUre

Bucket List

Things Everyone Should Do At Least Once Every Year!

1 Go to a Drive-in theater

I've always been a big fan of movie classics and love hearing my grandmother tell stories from when she was younger. I love to learn about things young people did for fun back in the day and makes me wonder what future generations will come up with. Yesterday... watching movies from your vehicle, today... Netflix®, tomorrow... movies will come in pill form! I don't know what I've been smoking, but I better take another hit. Weeee!

2 Go out Dancing

Dancing is a beautiful expression of the joy and freedom we gift to our souls. Unless you are drunk and taught to believe you are a very talented stripper right before hearing "last call" at the local bar! You don't have to be a professional dancer. Just go out there and let go! You know that expression that advises us to dance like no one is watching? Let them watch! But charge upfront for that show you're about to put on.

3 Sports Bar

I'm not a huge sports fan, but I've had a great time in these venues. The sense of camaraderie is amazing! You are bound to make instant friends simply because you are rooting for the same team playing on TV. You would even let a complete stranger drive your car when you've drank too much and let him marry your daughter simply because they are a "giraffes' fan" (or whatever animal the team you love has chosen for a mascot).

4 Theme Parks

You want to feel like a kid again? Go to a theme park and ride all the rides with friends and family. Take pictures with people dressed as famous fun characters, eat and laugh to your heart's content, borrow any item from any of the stores and run outside without paying for it to encourage security guards to play "catch me if you can" with you. Then break out of jail for a spirited game of "hide & seek!" Then join the police officers in a game of "catch the bullet"... then... You know what? Feel free to take a seat. I don't think you'll be in the mood to play anything anymore. Just be sure to ride a rollercoaster before you get into this mess! There is no greater rush than that!

5 Paddle Boats

There are many places with beautiful lakes that often have vendors with paddle boats. Some are in the shape of an animal like swans or ducks. Talk about taking a worry-free and relaxing trip across the lake on the calm waters surrounded by beautiful greenery, trees and flowers everywhere! It is a lovers' world and dogs' playground. So wonderful… so enchanting… until it pours rain all over your relaxed unsuspecting self.

6 Special Interests Museum

I've always loved going to museums. I love art & science museums like the Museum of Natural History in NY or the Museo de Arte in Ponce, PR. But there are also so many other wonderful museums that are truly one of a kind. For example, there is the Ripley's Believe it or Not Museum showcasing the greatest and most interesting array of oddities. There's also the Museum of Bad Art, Museum of Death, Museum of the Weird, the Underwater Museum in Mexico, Museum of Broken Relationships, and there are even museums based on a food item such as SPAM®, bananas and potatoes. I am sure you will find many other interesting museums to explore and learn from.

7 Murder Mystery Dinners

There's a restaurant I went to in Orlando where they serve the most amazing food while enjoying a very entertaining sleuth's show. It was dinner theater at its best in which we had to determine who was responsible for the murder of one of the characters. The audience was asked to participate at times, and it was quite comical. They also sell this concept in box sets for you to host your own murder mystery dinner experience in your home! I've hosted 6 so far and I am definitely hosting many more in the future. It's such a thrill to see your friends and family dressed up like the characters indicated in their invitations, follow their scripts while in character, enjoying a great dinner and seeing them as they go all over your house searching for clues to find out "who murdered who". Just don't make me cook. If I do cook, then you'll know it was me… in the dining room… with the pot roast. Mystery solved!

8 Nude Beach

Have you ever been nude in public? I have done this many times. Although, because people expect you to be nude in certain beaches, I find these to be less scandalous than walking down the street naked. In ancient Rome, men would gather inside bathhouses disrobed making it impossible to determine who belongs to what social class or what profession they exercised. They were all equal. I don't think this is the same reason why there are bathhouses and nude beaches nowadays, but I know many naturists frequent these. Many of us have bodily insecurities and are under so much pressure to look a certain way or are careful to hide physical imperfections we are ashamed of. Let go of all that nonsense! Skin to the wind! Or go skinny dipping in the lake without the man in the hockey mask with a machete waiting for you to come out of the water.

9 Game Night

This goes hand in hand with the feeling of being kids again. When we are kids, we play. When we are adults, we keep playing, but the games change, and the rules are different. We play games like "Guess if I'm Sad or Not" based on my posts in social media or "Let's See Who Has More Money, the Biggest House and the Greatest Car". Games before were a lot simpler. Get a group of friends to join you for a night of boardgames, video games or virtual reality games. Card games used to be all the rage back in the day. What happened? Go ahead: get together and play all night long!

10 Ride a Train

I don't mean subway trains. I'm referring to good old fashion locomotives! Some of these include meals and other perks. Some long trips offer the option of renting bedding space, and you wouldn't want to miss out on the wonderful scenery outside the windows! It's a beautiful way to travel across country while enjoying a view you wouldn't get from an airplane window.

11 Travel More

We always make travelling a resolution to accomplish every year, but we never get to. There are ways to do this and still be financially responsible. We just have to search for ways to make this possible. The world is so much greater than what we are accustomed to knowing in our own "backyard". These are my favorite in terms of exotic foods, majestic architecture, and the wonderfully colorful folklore such as the music, the people, clothing and history: Spain, Japan, The Caribbean, Dubai, Paris, Mexico, Egypt and in our American soil… California, New York, Nevada and Florida. Air B&B's are gaining more popularity these days as they offer a very affordable option as far as accommodations go. Join the Samba Parade in Brazil, Bathe in Iceland's Blue Lagoon, ride a gondola in Italy, see the Coliseum in Rome, see the pyramids in Machu Pichu (Peru), see Dracula's Castle in Romania and visit the Statue of Liberty in Manhattan!

12 Comic Con

I just realized a lot of the things I encourage have a lot to do with being a kid again. I am either very in touch with the child inside of me or I am extremely immature! Going to comic book conventions like Comic Con or Mega Con (all across the US) are fun ways to pay tribute to heroes, villains and even famous personalities in the science-fiction industry. You will find actors, movie directors, writers, illustrators, and animators from many different reputable companies. Not to mention, it is a great excuse to dress up without having to wait for Halloween! Cosplay, short for "costume play," is a very popular Japanese art where participants dress as their favorite movie, comic book, or video game characters, mimicking everything from their clothes to accessories and hairstyles to makeup, right down to their mannerisms and personalities!

13 Make a Haunted House

We all have fond childhood memories of this one house we all loved to go to every Halloween night because of the creative ways it was decorated. Every Halloween, my sister invites me to go out trick or treating with her kids around the neighborhood. There is one particular house that always stands out because of the spooky way it is decorated. I've always wanted to be "the Joneses" every month of October so I would wait for Halloween to be over, buy Halloween décor after they're put on sale, and decorate the house with these the following year. I would even encourage friends to hide in different areas of the house to scare unsuspecting neighbors who were invited to step inside in exchange for a nice dinner the weekend after. It was a very costly favor at times. Let your imagination run wild as you create the perfect Halloween house with an experience to die for!

14 Weather-Specific Sports

You should try activities that are usually attached to a specific type of weather. This is particularly enticing to people from colder climates who always wanted to try jet-skiing, snorkeling, hiking, go on nature walks or attend water parks and beaches across the country. The same can be said for people from hotter climates who always wanted to ski in the snow, go ice-skating, snowboarding or have a snowball fight. The spring has many floral-themed parades and the fall has the best leaves we gather to make mounts of them to jump into, not to mention delicious pumpkin-flavored items to consume and the most fashionable clothes.

15 Learn a New Language or Skill

Learning something new is always fun and a great way to stay smart and multi-talented. Growing up, I always witnessed how my mother would always raise her hand evert time someone asked "is there a doctor in the house"? It gave her such a great feeling of accomplishment and who doesn't like to feel needed, wanted or reliable? I wanted the same for myself, so I decided to never live the same day twice. I learned many skills and worked as an Event & Wedding Coordinator, Case Manager for a mental health facility, Program Coordinator for several support groups, Sales & Catering manager for hotels, Banquet Captain, Comedic Columnist for a local magazine, Sales & Marketing Manager and Caped Crusader on the weekends (in my head). We only live once, so why not do it all, be everything! Learn how to paint, play a musical instrument, learn a new language, do arts & crafts, practice archery, martial arts, how to renovate an area in your home or garden, how to cook, etc. The sky is the limit…unless you want to learn how to fly a plane! Then there really is no stopping you!

16 Run a Marathon or Triathlon

A triathlon is a multiple-stage competition involving the completion of 3 continuous and sequential endurance disciplines. Modern-day triathlons are swim/bike/run events that are done in that order. If you think that a marathon is tough, wait till you try a triathlon! Training and completing a marathon will not only help you develop your physical strength and endurance, but also your mental persistence, will, and attitude. I've participated in Disney marathons® myself. So much fun and yet another reason for me to wear a silly costume!

17 Extreme Sports

Some of these include skydiving, parasailing, parachuting, rafting, snowboarding, bungee jumping, climbing, windsurfing, paintball, etc. I do recommend everyone to try at least one extreme sport in our lifetimes! (Of course, make sure safety precautions are in place and you are with professional and licensed instructors.) While the experience may only last a couple of minutes, those few minutes will be some of the most memorable ones in your life.

18 Connect with People from Your Past

In our life's journey, we are constantly touched and supported by people around us, be it friends, family, or acquaintances. Can you identify someone who has made a difference in your life? Write a letter to that person today and let him/her know how much he/she means to you. You can do this as many times as you want, for as many people as you like. Think about your past teachers or those who served as parental guides. Find ways to get back in touch with them. (Calling your alma mater is always a good start.) Let them know how they have touched your life.

19 Mentor someone

Many communities are always looking for volunteer mentors, so check with your local community programs for such opportunities. At the same time, is there anyone you know who can benefit from being mentored by you? Extend your hand to help — who knows, it may well be what he/she needs at this moment! Making a difference is more than doing a kind deed, though it can come as a result of a kind deed. When you make a difference in someone's life, you change the person's life for the better… permanently. What is the difference YOU want to make in others' lives? How can you make that happen?

20 Befriend a Stranger

Buy someone's groceries, make a donation, do something that is kind in nature and encourage the recipients of these deeds to pay it forward and do good deeds onto others. If you're on a plane or at the bus or waiting in line, encourage someone to join you in conversation. Every person is an island… a new book to be read. There is so much we can learn from one another when we share our life's experiences. One time, during my college years, I approached a girl who was wearing a Batman shirt. I, as usual, was also wearing a Batman shirt. I told her I admired her taste in clothing and superheroes and then I asked her if she would join me for a cup of coffee. I told her it was something I liked to do every now and then as a social experiment in between classes. She agreed. We are STILL friends to this day! I even helped her coordinate her own wedding and our families became close friends as well. Because of this approach I can say, without a doubt, these people will always have a home in my house, and I will always have a home in their, which is (so far) 9 countries and multiple cities across the globe!

21 Dance in the Rain

We are all used to following a "proper" conduct: to be clothed when we are out, to always wear shoes when we are outside the house, and to always use an umbrella when it's raining (with good reason of course, so that we don't catch a cold). While all these make sense, how about breaking the "rules" for a change… and just walk… or even dance barefoot the next time it rains? Feel the pavement, feel the earth, and feel the wet surface against your feet. Better yet, find someone to do this with you. Get ready for a spontaneous burst of laughs!

22 Watch the Sun Rising or Setting

Sunrises and sunsets are some of the most beautiful gifts from mother nature. And the best thing? We get them *free* every day. Nothing like sipping a cup of coffee while being welcomed by the morning sun while you sit on the porch or saying farewell to another day with a glass of refreshing iced tea…while… sitting on the porch again? I seriously need to find other areas in the house to hang out.

23 See the Northern Lights

The Northern Lights, also known as the Aurora Borealis, is a "natural light display in the sky particularly in the high latitude (Arctic and Antarctic) regions, caused by the collision of energetically charged particles with atoms in the high-altitude atmosphere" (according to Wikipedia). The most popular places to see them are in Sweden, Iceland, Norway, Finland, Canada, and Scotland, though it should be noted that sightings are never guaranteed due to the unpredictability of weather. It is a breathtaking spectacle of lights when it does occur!

24 Whale Watching or Swimming with Dolphins

I am a huge lover of nature. Unless you're a mosquito. In that case, be afraid… be VERY afraid. I have never done either one, but I've always loved to. It's like being graced by nature itself and hearing a voice tell you "I love you. Everything is going to be OK. You are magnificent. You are an important part of all this beautiful world". Of course, hearing these could also mean I am in dire need of psychiatric assistance.

25 Plant Something and Watch it Grow!

I've always been a big fan of symbolisms. When visiting my grandmother's house, I hear so many stories that revolve around a tree she has there. I have seen so many pictures of my mother and her siblings when they were younger, pictures of me as a child and my sister's kids… all around or in front of that tree. That tree was planted by my grandfather and it's still there standing tall. To me, it isn't a tree anymore. It is symbolic of our family and how we have persevered throughout the years no matter what we have faced. We are still there, standing tall, providing shelter and sustenance to many creatures and shade or protection to those we love.

26 Inspire Others

Do you have something to say to others? Maybe an ability you have and would like to share? Perhaps you know of a better way to teach us something with ease? Go viral (social media or YouTube), attempt to speak in public or write a book about this! There are many ways to get your message across. Go ahead! What would you like to share with all of us? We are listening!

27 Go on a Road Trip

A road trip is a journey taken on roads, typically by automobile. While some would consider a road trip as tiring, a road trip can actually be fun, especially when accompanied by the right people — and perhaps, great music! Not only is it relaxing to go on a long, non-stop ride, it also provides a great view of the country/city (depends on where you are driving) and creates an opportunity for you and your companions to bond with each other.

28 See a Fortune Teller

Have you ever had your palm read or had a tarot card reading? A lot of us are fascinated with knowing what's ahead. What will out future be like? Although it is encouraged people see these as recreational activities, many do take these visions seriously. Who knows? Maybe they are. I've always seen them as an opportunity to reflect on my own life and try to see what things I need to do or change to obtain these desired visions for the future.

29 Create a Tradition

Go out to dinner and watch a movie on Fridays, wear blue on Wednesdays at work, have Martini Mondays with friends, visit family every other month (take turns on the family you're visiting if you're a couple). I have my own traditions: I watch a scary movie every Friday the 13th of any month. My ex and I would take turns in the kitchen (cooking and doing the dishes) on assigned days of the week and always had a date night every Sunday night. There is a sense of belonging and happiness in the normalcy of a routine or premeditated tradition between friends, family members or lovers. Of course, you should always leave some room for spontaneity! Can you come up with more fun traditions?

30 Volunteer Work

I cannot begin to tell you how rewarding volunteer work is! I've always said we all need each other in life. We may be strangers to one another, but we are all human beings on this planet trying to be happy and achieve many goals for ourselves and our families and friends. So, why can't we be there for one another? Doctors need car mechanics, mechanics need teachers for their children, teachers need cooks to prepare their meals at a restaurant, cooks need plumbers to fix plumbing issues in their homes, plumbers need people to pick up their garbage, people who gather our garbage need pilots to fly the planes they travel in to visit relatives, etc. I used to volunteer at the animal shelter after making sure it was the kind that didn't kill their animals after not being adopted for a long period of time. I've always wanted to volunteer at a hospice, but I am so emotional! It probably doesn't matter, but I would hate to have my emotions get the best of me. A hospice is a place of care for the terminally ill, in their final months/weeks. While we can't do anything about the patients' condition, what we can do is to provide emotional and spiritual support to them in their last days. Consider volunteering at a hospice — not only will you change the lives of the patients and their loved ones, but you may also well change your life in the process too.

31 Conquer your Fears

Franklin D. Roosevelt once said, "The only thing we have to fear is fear itself—nameless, unreasoning, unjustified terror which paralyzes needed efforts to convert retreat into advance." We all have fears. Fear of heights, fear of spiders, fear of speaking in public, fear of specific animals, fear of failure, and fear of rejection are among them. While physical fears are legitimate for safety reasons (fear of lions, fear of falling off a ledge, fire etc.), in most cases, our fears are irrational and don't protect us from any real danger. The good news is that fears can be overcome. Some fears (such as intense fear of dogs) can be a result of **traumatic events in the past**, while other fears (such as fear of failure and fear of rejection) can be simply a desire to protect ourselves from "danger" when the danger is merely self-perceived.

32 Forgive Someone

Unless you've lived a shielded life, chances are you've had conflicts with people before. Conflicts are never pleasant, sometimes resulting in soured or even broken friendships. But it doesn't have to end there. As Lewis Smedes said, "To forgive is to set a prisoner free and discover that the prisoner was you." Is there anyone whom you had conflicts with before? Is it time to let go and forgive him/her? While it may be difficult to let go of incidents where the person hurt you very deeply, remember that when you bear a grudge against someone, the person who gets hurt the most is you and not the other person, because you are the one bearing the "hate" and carrying its weight. Be the better man/woman: reach out, speak to the person, and bury the hatchet. You may be surprised at what comes out of it.

33 Fly in a Helicopter or Air Balloon

Who hasn't fantasized about flying before? Unlike a plane that sends you about 30,000 feet above ground and brings you right to the clouds and into the skies, a helicopter hovers at about 1,000 feet above ground, hence giving you the opportunity to enjoy some really fantastic views on earth. Thanks to **Groupon®, you can get a helicopter adventure ride** at relatively affordable prices. If you have a special occasion coming up such as a wedding anniversary or a loved one's birthday or marriage proposal or you are simply looking for a way to spice up your weekend, this will be a great activity to try out! The same goes for hot air balloon rides and they are less noisy.

34 Tell People You Love Them

None of us chose the families we were born into, but this doesn't change the fact that we love each other. From being with us when we took our first step as a baby; to our first day at school;

to going through puberty; to our graduation day; to our wedding day, our families have always been silently working behind the scenes to help us get through our lives in one piece.

Given that our families and some of our friends have always been there for us, it's always easy to take their presence for granted. How many of us have neglected our friends and family for work before? I know I have — and that's because my thinking is, "work is urgent, but friends and family will always be there tomorrow. After all, they've always been there, so I can postpone seeing them today".

But that is precisely the wrong kind of thinking — a thinking that takes things for granted. Life is short — you will never know when things disappear for the most unexpected reasons. No matter how busy you are, always make sure to set time for friends and family every day. Give them a call just to say you love them (you'll really surprise them). Give your mom and dad a peck on the cheek before you leave for work. Let them know that no matter how busy you are, they will always come first to you. You could at least bring yourself to hug people more often.

35 Go Cruising

Going on a cruise is an experience unlike any other. It's like being aboard a city on water! If you think you may get bored on board, then throw those thoughts off the deck because cruise companies offer various entertainment choices on board nowadays! From karaoke to mini-concerts, movie screenings, arcades, a great array of shops, meeting new people and the always unavoidable buffets!

36 Be of Service to Others

We live in a service-oriented world today, with restaurant servers, cashiers, call center staff, customer support centers, and retail assistants at our beckoning. While service staff is everywhere, it's certainly not an easy job. From unreasonable customers to weird customers, there are all kind of people in this world!

Yet, customer service can be fun and rewarding. I'm listing this down as a bucket list idea to consider because not only is it a tremendous personal growth experience, it puts you right at the intersection of people contact — where you interact with people face-to-face (or voice-to-voice if you're in a call center) and have the power to impact them and change their lives. Consider doing this, even if for a short duration — and you may find yourself a changed person after that who will always show appreciation to others every day of your life. I never knew the true meaning of patience, compassion, and determination until I became a server!

37 Recreate Old photos

Have you seen people recreate childhood photos as adults? Talk about an amazing gift for a parent! Surprise mom with a photo of you (or accompanied by your siblings) recreating the same pose you had years ago when you were kids. Make sure to wear the same exact replica of what it was worn in the photo back in the day and it helps if the background matches as well!

38 Fall in Love

To get things straight — you don't need to be in a relationship to be happy! That being said, the media often hypes up the notion of "finding your soulmate," "being in love," and "happily ever after," like being in a relationship with someone is the answer to all life's problems. However, to meet the right person who shares similar values as you, supports you in your life endeavors, and loves you unconditionally — this is one of probably one of the best things that can ever happen to anyone. The trick is not to find someone who completes you. You need to work on being a complete person and find another complete individual, so you can learn from one another and complement each other in many ways. It can be a boyfriend, girlfriend, spouse, best friend or family member.

So, get out there and date freely! Open your heart and mind and allow yourself to fall in love. Who knows, "the one" for you may well be around the corner and perhaps, reading this same book!

39 Go to a Concert

According to the dictionary, music is the art of arranging sounds in time to produce a composition through the elements of melody, harmony, rhythm and timbre. There is nothing like losing yourself in a melody as it surrounds your entire body making it almost impossible to hear anything else. Your body and soul are possessed by music and it is a wonderful experience. It is one of the few times I've actually said I could fill my entire body be filled with art! There are many outdoor concerts such as Burning Man that provide almost religious experiences. I have been to many rock concerts in my days and bonding with others around you becomes an easy task. There is also the beautiful musicality of the opera concertos and ballet recitals. Dare to be consumed by this art!

40 Go Out More... Live Life!

I've always said I don't like to live a life of regrets. I never want to find myself on my deathbed feeling bad because I never got to try something. This is why I try to experience as many things as I can from life before this is taken away from me. Unless that is committing armed robbery or murder. I'm pretty sure I can part without these. But what about comedy clubs, restaurants, horseback riding, surfing, nightclubs, escape rooms, fresh fruit picking, gather with friends and family around a campfire, or any of the things mentioned previously on this list? How about adopting a pet? Let me tell you something… the best lessons in life I have learned from dogs I've owned. My last dog died of cancer and had lost his eyesight. He was always in pain because of arthritis, but always wagged his tail happily when he heard my voice. Every dog I've had had been incredibly loyal to me in exchange for a name and a bowl of food and water. Do you want to see what happiness looks like? Look in the eyes of a dog who you've adopted and play with every day! Adopt an animal today and make it your friend for life!

Here are some more I found online. Can you think of more?

See volcanos in activity / wine tasting / go on a hunt for the Loch Ness Monster, Big Foot, aliens, ghosts or anything else that is considered a myth / visit the White House / ride a motorcycle / meditate / learn magic tricks / get married / become a parent / get your dream job / prepare a will / swim in bioluminescent water / take underwater pictures / go to a circus / see a Broadway musical / see a major sport event live like Wimbledon, the Super Bowl or basketball game / set a record / stop procrastinating / read more / exercise / finish a goal!

_____

_____

_____

_____

_____

_____

_____

_____

_____

_____

_____

_____

In Conclusion...

This concludes The L Word. I'm sure many more things will happen that will make me laugh, learn something or love something which I will want to share with the world. For this reason, it was hard to end this chapter in my life, but I needed to publish this now because people need to laugh now more than ever! We had a rough year with the pandemic and many other things that made life more challenging for us. I'm sure there will be a sequel to this book and maybe a lot more books of this nature because that is life. Life keeps on going and I will always find things I will want to share with the world to make you all as happy as these experiences have made me. Remember that a smile on your face is our way of telling the world "is that the worst you can do"?

Keep on laughing, learning, living, loving and luring others into joining you in many exciting adventures!

I want to thank my family for being so supportive every time I've found myself struggling with life. Humor has helped me a lot to survive many difficult situations, but I would never have made it as far as I've come without your love and support. Thank you, mother (Dr. Dulce Rodríguez), my sister (Dulce Perez), my grandmother (Dulce Estrella), my cousin Katherine Berroa, my aunt Dorka Rodriguez, the wonderful and always beautiful Tita De Despradel and her wonderful family, and my aunt/guardian angel Tuti (Niurka Rodriguez) for sharing your lives with me during this horrible pandemic we all experienced and for making me laugh so much!

I also want to thank a special person I met during this pandemic, Raith Breuer (my Irish Hulk and "hunny bunny"). Because of this obligated distancing, we have yet to meet in person, but it was a blessing getting multiple calls from you every day. Thank you for making me smile, believe in love and have hope for the future. I cannot wait to spend the rest of my life with you. Thank you for your faith in me and making this "superhero" believe there are heroes in his life as well.

Friends were God's consolation prize during this pandemic, and I consider myself very lucky to have the friends I have. Thank you for the hours of entertainment, laughter and keeping each other in good spirits and eager to fight adversity! Many thanks to Paul Bradford (my brother from another mother) and his husband Paul Martin (my Brit). The thoughtful David and Amanda Bradford. My particularly good friends and extended family Ayr Poucher and Gail Kimball. The hilarious and expressive Andrew Vance Meade. Collette MacNicol (my very funny and creative Girl Scout cookies liaison). Cat Castoro (my beautiful Wonder Woman). My cutie patootie friend Rhona Noguera. The visionary Pierce Hanson. The very talented Nigel Revenge. Eric Beaulieu (the real-life Prince Charming). Alfonso Forment (my second dad). The sweet Ryan Carter Smith. My very interesting array of funny, informative and somewhat dirty social media buds: Alex Costa, Alberto Fernandez Sabater, Johnathan Greenfield, and Nicholas Machado. Reina Nunez (my sister from another mister). The insanely funny and beautiful Gatica Felina Glez. The very strong and inspiring Sydney Bermudez. Richie Medina and his witty/very humorous posts on social media. Lorenzo Fernandez Garciadiego for his delicious contributions (from the U Can Cook team in Orlando). My fellow superhero Michael Wickham from 321 No Fault. My very talented graphic artist Ludwig Galvis. Carmen Paredes (you'll always be my other mom). Rony Sada (thank you for so many years of friendship and for still sticking around in spite of my craziness).

Last, but certainly not least, I want to thank you, my dear reader. Holding this book in your hands is testimony of your support. You are the reason why I wake up every day wanting to smile and share something humorous with the world. If I've made you smile today, please share this with others. Help me fill this world with laughter one person at a time and help me create a much better world to live in.

From the bottom of my heart…

THANK YOU!!!

About the Author

Jerry Perez is a loser! At least this is what he thought when he was forced to return home to be with his mother after the pandemic we all suffered in the year 2020 robbed him of his career as an event/wedding coordinator, his home, his previous loving relationship, his friends... his whole life changed. Luckily, this only made him work harder to turn something negative into something positive for him and all those who surround him. He turned to humor to create this book in the hopes others could look at the brighter side of things when life gets a little hard to handle.

Mr. Perez began his journey as a published horror-fiction writer in the year 2010 when he released *City of Shadows* and *Shadow Ville (2012)*. He then worked for a local magazine in South Florida where he was in charge of the comedic column for this publication. He then suffered a car accident which robbed him of his memories causing him to live with both retrograde and anterograde amnesia (no recollections of his life before the accident and making it harder to retain new information). As soon as he taught himself how to write again, he decided to publish another book relating his experiences with this mental health condition in the hopes he could help others like him suffering from any kind of dementia (from Alzheimer's disease to any other types of memory loss), so that no one would ever have to feel as lonely and vulnerable as he once felt. This book is titled *I Forgot to Remember (2020)*.

The L Word (2021) is this writer's 4th piece of work, but far from being his last.

Notes:

Made in the USA
Columbia, SC
08 June 2021